Molly:

Here's that treasure
chest of well-turned
phrases and very "good lines"
I promised you. You can
pick and choose and blend
topics and ideas; so don't
be limited by the Table of
Contents — read the whole
thing.

Trusting that this will do
you as much good as it
has for me (even though not by
a Jesuit) and wishing you
all the best with the "roundball"
and the "hard heads," I am

John Clark

P.S. Regards to his America!

WORDS OF POWER

WORDS OF POWER

Religious Invocations and Addresses

by

James E. McNulty, OSA

Edited by George F. Riley, OSA

ALBA HOUSE · NEW YORK

SOCIETY OF ST. PAUL, 2187 VICTORY BLVD., STATEN ISLAND, NEW YORK 10314

WORDS OF POWER

Religious Invocations and Addresses

by

James F. McNulty, OSA

Edited by George F. Riley, OSA

ALBA · HOUSE   NEW · YORK

SOCIETY OF ST. PAUL, 2187 VICTORY BLVD., STATEN ISLAND, NEW YORK 10314

Library of Congress Cataloging in Publication Data

McNulty, James F., d. 1979
  Words of power.

  1. Occasional sermons. 2. Catholic Church—
Doctrinal and controversial works—Catholic authors—
Addresses, essays, lectures. 3. Prayers. I. Riley,
George F. II. Title.
BV4254.2.M38   1982   252'.02   83-2514
ISBN 0-8189-0442-9

Nihil Obstat:
Daniel V. Flynn, J.C.D.
Censor Librorum

Imprimatur:
†Joseph T. O'Keefe
Vicar General,
Archdiocese of New York

Designed, printed and bound in the United States of
America by the Fathers and Brothers of the
Society of St. Paul, 2187 Victory Boulevard,
Staten Island, New York 10314, as part of their
communications apostolate.

2 3 4 5 6 7 8 9 (Current Printing: first digit)

TABLE OF CONTENTS

DEDICATION

Kärntrer-Ring is a major boulevard in Vienna, Austria; it is an avenue of beauty in one of the world's most enchanting cities. But on December 30, 1978 it became a scene of horror for my close friend and associate, the Rev. James F. McNulty, O.S.A.

When Father Jim was crossing the broad boulevard on that December day, he was struck down by a speeding metro liner. He died ten days later in a Vienna hospital. To this day I have trouble believing this tragic event actually happened.

For fifteen years he and I collaborated in writing, drafting and exchanging sermons, benedictions, homilies, invocations, and major addresses that we had given as priests in the Augustinian Order.

It is perhaps not fair to say collaborating, for Father Jim was one of the most respected and gifted retreat masters in the order. He was splendidly eloquent as a speaker and as a writer his skill was unmatched. Whatever talents I brought to our collaboration were minor compared to the gifts of this giant of a spiritual communicator.

By the sheerest coincidence, only months before his death, he had placed in my hands all of the personal manuscripts of notes and writings undertaken during his apostolate as a retreat master.

Following his death I made a vow that someday those beautiful and inspiring talks, together with those I had done over a similar period, would find their way into print. I felt I

owed that to Father Jim, because whatever talents I developed
were the result of my good fortune to be associated with him.

In addition, Father McNulty's loving parents, Mr. and
Mrs. Frank A. McNulty of Andover, Mass., were a motivating
force in the preparation of this publication. Father Jim's works
appear herein with his parents' permission and blessing.

It is with a sense of accomplishment and gratitude that I
dedicate this book to the memory of the Rev. James McNulty,
O.S.A., fellow Augustinian, loyal friend, and one of Christ's
surest, truest messengers.

Rev. George F. Riley, O.S.A.

ACKNOWLEDGMENTS

Grateful acknowledgment is made to the following authors and publishers for permission to use material under their copyright:

"What Kind of Fool Am I?" from musical production *Stop the World I Want to Get Off*. Words and music by Leslie Bricusse and Anthony Newley. Copyright 1961 TRO Essex Music Ltd., London. Used with permission of TRO-Ludlow Music, Inc., New York.

"The Impossible Dream," by Mitch Leigh and Joe Darion, Copyright 1965 Andrew Scott, Inc., Helena Music Corporation. Used with the permission of Alan S. Honig, Administrator.

Father McNulty was an admirer of the inspirational books of Rev. Joseph R. Manton, *cssr*, and often quoted his writings as preaching aids. Readers may recognize in this work word images which are the result of Father McNulty's fascinations with the Manton writings. Formal thanks is also given to Rev. John A. Aherne, *osa*, former president of Merrimack College, Massachusetts, Rev. G.P. Lawless, and Rev. Milton Jordon for scattered contributions which were adapted by the author, and to Linda Delaney.

Part I

Invocations and Blessings

GRADUATION INVOCATIONS/BLESSING

Heavenly Father, we ask the blessing of your love on all present here for this happy occasion; on the faculty and administration, and all those in the _____ community who have pooled and shared their resources, talent, time, and energy to help these graduates reach this day; on parents and friends who have sacrificed for and given support to them on their journey; on the graduates themselves for whom today represents a reward of long hours of hard, tedious, and often lonely work.

Bless this newest generation of hope with the grace to know your will and the courage to follow it; the strength to lift the City of Man to the City of God; the intelligence to do what is right because it is right, in a world of confusion and compromise; the insight to accept your truth in a world that rejects it; the humility to realize that love of power forever threatens the power of love.

Lord Jesus, carpenter of Nazareth, you were young once as these graduates are. May our world be better for their having been here, as Christian moral principles and priorities are reflected and reinforced in their future lives. Let them not live in a world different from others, but rather let them live in the same world differently, looking to you for guidance in the midst of confusion, strength in time of despair, wisdom in the face of indecision. This, your blessing, we ask in the name of the Father, and of the Son, and of the Holy Spirit.

BENEDICTION

Lord God, giver of all good gifts, we thank you for your

bountiful blessings. We are especially grateful today for the success of these graduates whose accomplishments give great promise for the enrichment—intellectual, social, and moral—of your kingdom on earth.

Instill into the hearts of these graduates sentiments of gratitude to their parents, appreciation of their instructors, loyalty to their schoolmates, love for their alma mater, and, most of all, the grace to conduct themselves always according to the ideals and truths of the one Church of Christ.

Grant your grace, O God, and the fulfillment of all the just hopes and lofty aspirations of these young men and women. We beg of you, our sovereign and supreme Lord, an abundance of blessings upon this assembly, upon our families and friends, upon our church and country through your gracious goodness and the infinite merits of our Lord Jesus Christ.

PRE-MEAL INVOCATIONS

Father in heaven, you have made us for yourself and our hearts are restless till they rest in you.

Give us the virtue of courage . . .

. . . to realize that push-button solutions are an illusion.

. . . to stand up for our convictions no matter what the cost.

. . . to seek freedom with responsibility.

. . . to temper our lives with common sense.

. . . to appreciate what others have done for us.

Then will we understand the meaning of unity, truth, and charity, which tell us that this world can be one only if our unity is based on truth and experienced in love for one another.

Bless this food and those who provide it. As it feeds our bodies . . . may your friendship forever sustain our American heritage and us, her people. We ask this in Jesus' name.

God, our Father, we ask your blessing of love on all here present.

Give us the strength to bring the city of man back to the city of God, so that the paradise we lost may, through you, become paradise regained.

Give us the intelligence to know ourselves, that we may better know you, whose wisdom is ever ancient and ever new.

Give us the humility to know that the love of power will forever threaten the power of love.

Give your blessing to our families and friends so that the food we share and the bread we break may strengthen us to serve our nation well.

We ask this in Jesus' name.

POST-MEAL INVOCATIONS

Lord God, as we come to the twilight of this wonderful evening, our thoughts of gratitude as always return to you, the giver of life and love, sanity and sanctity.
The food we have eaten is now a part of us.
The laughter we have shared is now a part of us.
The words we have spoken are now a part of us.
The faith we profess is always a part of us.

As we again depart for that mysterious road of day to day reality, may we all enjoy . . .
. . . economic success in terms of security,
. . . physical success in terms of health,
. . . spiritual success in terms of peace.

May we always remember your immortal plea for unity, truth, and charity, which assures us that we will be one, when our unity is based on God's truth and experienced in his love.

Heavenly Father, we make our prayer of gratitude as brothers and sisters of your Son Jesus who lives with you and the Holy Spirit.

We know, God, that gratitude is a neglected virtue in today's world. So many of us neglect to say "Thank you" for your blessings. In the rush to secure and maintain the rights so freely talked about today, let us remember that all of these rights are gifts from you. Without you, your guidance, your direction, and your meaning in our lives, we would accomplish nothing—and be nothing.

Tonight, therefore, we thank you for all your blessings on us, our families, friends, and country. We are grateful, not only for this meal this evening but for the food you provide for us throughout our lives. Help us to remember those less fortunate than us in material and spiritual ways.

We have dined with friends. Let us remember that even as your food has nourished our bodies, so too may your graces and these friendships feed our souls.

Good night, good-bye, Godspeed, and God bless you always.

As the curtain goes down on this festive evening, we return to you, O heavenly Father, in a spirit of humility and gratitude for your myriad gifts and favors. You have taught us that life need not consist of restlessness without reasonableness, and process without prudence. May we always remember to pray that as Americans we will bless and profess God before we lustily sing, "God Bless America."

May we always be aware of the difficulties, differences, and needs of our neighbors. May we, "as we hunger and thirst after justice," have regard for the hunger and thirst of all peoples both at home and abroad.

May we have "compassion on the multitude," upon the people who really need people.

We have so much to give, for we Americans are the most fortunate people in the world.

We ask for a spirit of generosity in the name of your generous Son, Jesus.

SPECIAL OCCASION INVOCATIONS

WEDDING DINNER INVOCATION

Lord Jesus Christ, our Savior and Friend, before sitting down at our banquet tables this evening, we want prayerfully to invoke your holy name.

We are especially happy to make this prayer now, Lord, because we are not in church nor even in trouble. Rather we are ready for an evening of pleasure and relaxation. You know, Lord, as a rule when we speak to you, we are either kneeling against the background of a stained glass window or else buckling on a life preserver.

But this evening is gloriously different. We want you to bless our joy as we stand in glowing health, poised for a few hours of genial festivity. We even hope that, as you once tapped your miraculous power to fill the empty "Wine Jugs" at Cana and kept a marriage feast going merrily on, so tonight you will deign to bless this congenial company and keep our merriment going happily on.

Bless us then, Lord, and, in thy goodness, grant that the food be well-flavored, the service smooth, the humor rich, the singing true, and (if this isn't asking too much) the speeches short. May we sit down hungry and hopeful; may we rise satisfied and thankful and leave this evening more friendly toward our brothers and sisters, and more aware of what we owe you, our Friend and Savior.

INVOCATION FOR A BUSINESS LEADER

O God, our loving Father, we ask your blessing on all here present. Tonight we honor a friend, a businessman dedicated to the business of the common man. In so doing, we honor ourselves for having such a friend.

And yet, sad to say, we tend to forget you and your many goodnesses.

We live in an age afflicted with an obsession for speaking out and an aversion for thinking through.

We live in an age of the vocal minority that gleefully boasts of controlling nature but is unable to achieve self-control.

But this evening is gloriously different.

We are gathered here to pay tribute to a man and friend.

A man who has set a standard of excellence for us to emulate.

A man who is forever a realist, his acute mind uncluttered by cobwebs of vagueness.

A man who is a student of living, a builder, and a battler.

More than a century ago, Abraham Lincoln, sixteenth president of the United States, prayed: "Give our nation a clear vision, O Lord, that we may know where to stand and what to stand for, because unless we stand for something, we will fall for anything."

Lord, grant your blessings to our great American republic, our families, and our friends.

May we sit down hungry and hopeful and rise up satisfied and thankful.

May we leave this evening more friendly to all people and more aware of our debt to you, our heavenly Father.

INVOCATION AT POLICE & FIREMEN COMMUNION BREAKFAST

Lord Jesus Christ, our Savior and Friend, we are especially happy to offer this prayer to you, because today we are with a group of wonderful people, men and women who are a living rebuttal to that oft-heard exclamation, "What's Wrong

With America?" True, our age may seem to be afflicted with an obsession for speaking out and an aversion to thinking through. But look at these members of the _____. They do not represent what is wrong with America. Not of such mettle are the dedicated men and women standing reverently in your presence this morning. For them, you are not dead. For them, patriotism is not square. For them, virtue is not passe. They are the glorious answer to the question, "What's Right With America?"

So bless these, your civil servants, Lord. Grant wisdom to their minds, clearness to their thoughts, truth to their words, and love to their hearts. May they always set the interests of the community above those of the party; the interests of the nation above those of the community, and faithfulness to you above everything else.

INVOCATION AT A LAW SCHOOL

Almighty Father, supreme lawgiver, help all of us to understand, respect, and improve our American system of justice. As lawmakers, interpreters, enforcers, and observers, let us be just and merciful in our applications. We pray that the difficult and delicate balance between the rights of the individual and the society in which he or she lives be maintained, and that implementation of the one not detract from the other.

We ask for order and decorum in our courts, without which no true justice can prevail. Let not the unrest and disturbance of the moment bring about excessive harshness of penalty or extreme leniency of sentence.

With pardonable pride, may the administration, faculty, and students of this School of Law continue to be a shining example of these concepts to the legal profession.

Bless this food and those less fortunate in their repast this evening.

INVOCATION AT OPENING OF A NEW BUILDING

Father in heaven, we pray to you on this day when we dedicate this building for _____ (name of dep't).

We pray for all those who have made this day possible, for the faculty and students who have created and maintained a tradition of excellence, and for all those whose generosity and initiative have created this building.

We particularly pray for those who will be educated in this building.

Let them learn that you are the giver of every good gift on earth, in the sea, and in the sky,

that you bestow on man the intelligence and will to seek out the secrets of creation,

and that all knowledge leads to you.

Give the upcoming generations who will use this building courage . . .

. . . to stand up for their convictions no matter what the cost;

. . . to temper their lives with balance and good common sense;

. . . to appreciate what others have done before them;

. . . to pray;

. . . to live;

. . . to die and receive the divine accolade of "Well done, good and faithful servant."

Then will they understand the meaning of our motto, "Unitas, Veritas, Caritas," which tells us that this world can be one, if our unity is based on truth and experienced in love.

INVOCATION AT BANQUET HONORING ONE PERSON

Almighty God, giver of life, love, and liberty, we call upon you this evening to bestow your blessing on this annual dinner.

May the inspiration of _____'s care, concern, commitment, and charity be mirrored in our personal lives in this world of speed, power, confusion, and change.

May each of us bring the City of God to the City of Man, the love of the Heavenly City to the Inner City, so that we regard rightly the hunger and thirst after justice of all people as did that great and good person we honor here tonight.

Renew in our minds a knowledge of self, a knowledge of people and a knowledge of God whose wisdom, presence, and beauty are ever ancient and ever new.

Accordingly, we ask your blessing upon our families, friends, and foes and also upon these gifts we are about to receive from our opulent land. Tonight may we all come closer together in Christ.

INVOCATION AT ATHLETIC BANQUET

Almighty God, on this evening of _____ (name of school) annual football banquet, we ask your blessing on our nation, our school, our families, and our friends. May we follow the admonition and the footsteps of that spiritual athlete of the New Testament, St. Paul, to run a good race and to keep the faith.

Father, we pause for a time of mirth and merriment, of food and fun, to honor our athletes who have dedicated their time, talents, and skills to the great cause of _____ (name of school), the meaning factor of our lives and hopes. In that spirit we pray for your special blessings.

Bless, O Lord, our families with love,
> our country with peace,
> our souls with tranquility,
> our lives with balance and conviction.

We trust you, for without you nothing is real, nothing is strong, nothing has meaning.

In eating this meal, we pray for our city and our country, and we ask you to remind us to use the good things of this life to earn the blessing of your mystical vision for eternity.

Part II

Special Addresses

FUNERALS

EULOGY FOR A PRIEST

"There is an appointed time for everything,
   and a time for every affair under the heavens.
A time to be born and a time to die,
   a time to plant and a time to uproot the plant.
A time to weep and a time to laugh,
   a time to mourn and a time to dance.
A time to keep, and a time to cast away."
                                        (Ecclesiastes 3:1, 2, 4, 6)

"There is an appointed time for everything." We are here this morning, my dear friends, because one of these times has come. Father _____ (name) is dead. _____ days ago, there came to this kind, warmhearted priest a time to die. And we, his family, friends, and brothers in Christ gather together in this chapel to pay our homage. For us it is a time to mourn. A time to recall memories. A time to rearticulate answers to the perennial question of life and death.

Sigmund Freud said that death is the goal of all life, and Peter Pan saw it as an awfully big adventure. Socrates thought death might be the greatest of all human blessings, and contemporary theologians vie with each other to discourse learnedly on the subject of thanatology. Special ministries on death and dying swirl around us, and college courses are oversubscribed as they explore death's individual, social, and spiritual dimensions.

Yet, amidst all this interest in death, something is missing. There is an absence. How else could a respected medical doctor write in an equally respected medical journal these penetrating words: "In my opinion, death is an insult. It is the strangest, most unreasonable thing that can happen to a human being."

A startling sentence. Our instinctive reaction is to deny it outright. But let us permit Father _____ to deny it for us. For this morning, he preaches to us once more. By his death he answers two profound questions. What does it mean for a human person to die? What should it mean for a Christian to die?

By his death, Father _____ answers first the question: What does it mean for a human person to die? Some years ago, a Catholic philosopher penned some profound reflections on the death of his wife. One passage is particularly pertinent: "An animal or a pet is in some sense replaceable when it dies. But in the death of a person, there is a loss of something absolutely unique. When an animal dies, there is the loss of an *it*. When a human being dies, an *I* is lost to the world. A *thou* is lost to the survivors."

An *I* who will perhaps best be remembered as a kind man who brought laughter, mirth, and joy into people's lives through his sense of humor, his talent for song, his warm, expansive heart. An *I* who laughed and loved, worried and wept, danced and dreamed, sang and served, prayed and worked. This *I* is now lost to the world. This *I*, God will not, indeed cannot, replace. This *I* who touched a whole unique world with his warm flame of human living is dead.

This is the reason we are sad today. This is the reason we shed tears. This is the reason we are experiencing sorrow. It is a time to mourn. A human person has died. But Father_____ asks us not to stop here; he urges us to go further. To go beyond. It is one thing to state what it means for a human person to die. It is another to declare what it means for a Christian to die. And by his death, Father _____ answers also that second question: What does it mean for a Christian to die?

To answer this question, it is helpful to distinguish between purpose and meaning. Even though these two words are often used interchangeably, there is between them a delicate distinction insightfully portrayed by a prominent psychologist, Victor Frankl. Purpose, he remarks, is something functional; meaning, something personal. Purpose is something I do; meaning, something I am. Purpose is something I control, I command; meaning is something that controls me, that commands me.

All of us had a purpose in coming to this funeral Mass this morning. We came to pay homage to our relative, our brother, our friend. But we controlled the purpose. We did not have to come. In fact, until the moment we parked the car and then pushed open the chapel door, we controlled our coming. We were in charge of our purpose.

Once we entered the chapel, however, a change occurred. Our purpose ended. We had arrived. One hopes that meaning began to take over. The beauty of this Liturgy of the Resurrection, the presence of all these men and women who cared for Father _____, the support of our belief in Jesus—all these factors have reached out and taken hold of us.

This is why we can say that for a Christian, death has meaning. Granted, in death, life's purpose is finished. We can no longer control what happens. Granted, an *I* is lost to the world. For a human person, death is indeed death.

But for a Christian, death is life. Death takes on a meaning. For Father _____ has not died altogether, totally, utterly. That is a frightfully negative point of view. Father _____ has died and reached that unique point between time and timelessness when the Spirit of Christ has finally taken complete, permanent possession of him. Father _____ has died and entered into that extraordinary experience when

Christ, who is life, finally fashions him into his life. Truly in death, Father _____ has lost a purpose but found a meaning. A meaning intended to reach out to you, and you, and me.

Obviously this conviction compels a new attitude for us. We dare not be "resigned" to death. That is insufficiently Christian. We are still looking at death as the "enemy." In contrast, Karl Rahner insists that death should be an act we personally perform, not an experience we endure. Death is a yes, an "I do." When Jesus cried out with a loud voice, "Father, into your hands I commit my spirit," he was affirming life. And this is what a Christian proclaims with his last breath: "I have life. In death I shall find meaning."

Here is the message Father _____ preaches to us about death. Not enthusiasm, but readiness. Not surrender, but a love-filled yes. Not a human contest between life and purpose, but a Christian tension between life and meaning.

At its most profound level, this is the Christian meaning of death. This is the meaning Father _____ wishes us to take away from this, his funeral Mass. Because we are his family and friends and will miss him, it is a time to mourn. But because we are Christians, because we believe, it is a time for us, and above all, for Father _____, to rejoice.

Truly,

"There is an appointed time for everything,
    and a time for every affair under the heavens.
A time to be born and a time to die,
    a time to plant and a time to uproot the plant.
A time to weep and a time to laugh,
    a time to mourn and a time to dance.
A time to keep, and a time to cast away."

EULOGY FOR A SISTER

"Whether I live or whether I die, Christ will be exalted

through me. For, to me, life is Christ, and death is gain."
Philippians 1:20-21

This is a poignant occasion for me. Three weeks ago I preached the homily at Sister _____'s Golden Jubilee Mass. This morning I find myself preaching the eulogy at Sister _____'s funeral Mass. Oddly enough, there are normally two times when a Sister is preached about: at her profession (or anniversary thereof) and at her funeral. Is it a mere coincidence that in the space of _____ Sister _____ has been the subject of both these homilies? Is it sheer chance that just as at her Jubilee, Sister spoke eloquently to us of life, today she speaks brilliantly to us of death?

Beyond any doubt, death has today gained unprecedented prominence in modern American religion and culture. "The media is alive with death," says one seminary professor. "I have never seen so many newspaper and magazine articles, so many books and television programs focusing on the subject." How true! No one has to convince us that there is renewed attention to death among theologians. Or that special ministries relating to death and dying are growing. Or that college and high school courses in thanatology are exploring the individual and social dimensions of death.

Yet, amidst all this interest in death, something is missing. How else could a respected medical doctor write in a respected medical journal: "In my opinion, death is an insult. It is the strangest, most unreasonable thing that can happen to a human being."

A startling sentence. Our instinctive reaction is to deny it outright. But let us permit Sister _____ to deny it for us. Just as she taught us about life, so too at her funeral this morning she teaches us about death. In fact, by her death, Sister _____ answers first the question: What does it mean for a human person to die? A few years ago, a Catholic philosopher penned some profound reflections on the death of his wife. One passage is particularly pertinent: "An animal or a pet is in some sense replaceable when it dies. But in the death of a person, there is a loss of something absolutely unique. When an animal dies, there is the loss of an *it*. When a human being dies, an *I* is lost to the world. A *thou* is lost to the survivors."

An *I* who cradled Jesus Christ on her tongue and who gently held the hands of her Sisters. An *I* who laughed and loved, worried and wept, danced and dreamed, sang and sinned, prayed and worked. This *I* is now lost to the world. This *I*, God will not, indeed cannot, replace. This *I* who touched a whole unique world with her warm flame of human living is dead.

This is the reason we are sad today, and shed tears, and experience sorrow. A human being has died. But Sister _____ asks us not to stop here. She urges us to go further, go beyond. It is one thing to state what it means for a human person to die. But it is another to declare what it means for a Christian to die. And by her death, Sister _____ answers that second question: What does it mean for a Christian to die?

During the extensive television coverage of President Kennedy's funeral, a well-known news commentator came upon the phrase, "A Requiem Mass will be celebrated." He commented, "That can't be right!" The broadcast continued while the station phoned the Chancery Office in New York to verify the use of the word, "celebrate." Some minutes later the viewers were assured that this word was appropriate in describing the Catholic attitude toward death.

To my knowledge, Sister _____ never worked in the New York Chancery. But this morning she delivers to us the same message the Chancery official transmitted to that newscaster. The Christian attitude toward death is celebration.

True, in death an *I* is lost to the world. True, in death a *thou* is lost to the survivors.

Death is indeed death. But more importantly death is life. Sister _____ has not died altogether, totally, utterly. Sister _____ has died and reached that unique point between time and timelessness when the Spirit of Christ has finally taken complete, permanent possession of her. Sister _____ has died and entered into that extraordinary experience when Christ who is life finally fashions her to his life. Is it any wonder that St. Paul says, "For me, life is Christ, and death is gain!"

Obviously this conviction compels a new attitude for you and me. We dare not be "resigned" to death. That is insufficiently Christian. We are still looking at death as "the enemy." In contrast Karl Rahner insists that death should be an act we perform, not an experience we endure. Death is a yes, an "I do." When Jesus cried with a loud voice, "Father, into your hands I commit my spirit," he was affirming life. And this is what a Christian proclaims with his last breath: "I have life." Only with this attitude can death be an act I perform.

Here is the message Sister _____ preaches to us about death. Not enthusiasm, but readiness. Not surrender, but a love-laden yes. Not a human contest between life and death, but a Christian tension between life and life.

Some years ago, a 16-year-old girl lay dying in a Phoenix hospital. Her parish priest was a dear friend. The last time he saw the girl he must have looked dreadfully upset. The priest writes: "She looked up into my worried, harried face and said, 'Don't be afraid.' "

At its most profound level, this is the Christian meaning of death.

"Don't be afraid!"

A child can say it to an adult.

A girl can say it to a priest.

A deceased Sister can say it to living Religious. "Don't be afraid!" Sister _____ preached this message by her life. Now she preaches this message by her death. On the day of her Jubilee and on the day of her funeral, she says to us: "Don't be afraid!" "Whether I live or whether I die, Christ will be exalted through me. For, to me, life is Christ, and death is gain."

EULOGY FOR A TEACHING SISTER

"I firmly trust and anticipate that I shall never be put to shame for my hope; I have full confidence that now, as always, Christ will be exalted through me, whether I live or die. For, to me, 'life' means Christ; hence, dying is so much gain."

Philippians 1:20-21

In the new Order of the Mass, one prescription reads, "A homily, not a eulogy, is to be preached at funerals and other Masses for the dead."

How wise that is. After all, eulogies have a way of looking at what a person has done, what she has accomplished, what she has achieved. And we could preach a most eloquent eulogy for Sister _____ this morning. We could point out the years of witness that she gave as a Sister of _____. We could enumerate the hundreds of children that she influenced as a teacher in and out of her classroom. We could allude to the numerous adults that she inspired by her hard work and dedication. Yet, such a theme would only be a shallow tribute to Sister _____. Eulogizing what she did, we would skim over who she was. And it is this vibrant message of who she was that brings all of us here to _____ Church this morning. For to each and every one of us Sister _____ preaches a homily this morning. A homily of her joy as a Sister and as a woman of Christian hope.

In the silence of death, Sister _____ speaks to us this morning, first of all, of her joy as a Sister of _____. A famous theologian once remarked that a Religious is one who not only tells others what Christ says, but in a unique way, shows others who Christ is. A Religious not only delivers Christ's message, but also shapes his image. Such a statement seems especially tailored to Sister _____. In an age troubled by crises of identity, Sister _____ never doubted her own. She was a Religious committed to experiencing Christ, not addressing Christ. And that experiencing was particularly characterized by her membership in the Order of the _____.

In the silence of death, Sister _____ speaks to us also of her joy of Christian hope. All of us, I am sure, recognize that one of the major problems facing our world today is hopelessness. People are losing hope in their country, in their Church, even in themselves. The wars in Asia and Africa seem to be going on forever. Prices are rising despite the freeze. Unrest, riots, violence are still on the scene. Young people are turning away from Church and turning towards drugs. Years ago, I read a story of a young girl in London, England, who committed suicide. Her name was Samantha Clare. When they found her body and the empty bottle of sleeping tablets, they also found her diary in which she had written these lines: "I sit and dream for hours of things I would like to be. I would like to be Frank Sinatra's wife. I would like to be a fairy godmother. I would like to be a movie actress. I know none of these things are realistic, but I cannot face reality. How I wish someone would give me hope. I need hope."

Sister _____ recognized this need. She was above all a woman of hope. Everyone who visited her came away more hopeful, more full of confidence. I remember the afternoon that I invited Sister to address a room full of women gathered for a Day of Recollection. "What should I say to them, Father?" she asked. "Simply what you feel about God and how you are responding to this sickness." She talked to these women for forty-five minutes, and when I finally entered to break up the long session, the ladies were still enthralled. We ordinarily end our Days of Recollection with Benediction. I made this announcement but noticed the time was getting late. One woman remarked, "We don't need Benediction, Father. I saw Christ this afternoon, sitting in that wheelchair."

This is the hope that characterized the life of Sister _____. A hope that reaches its climax today as we celebrate her funeral Mass. Granted there are tears today—but did not Jesus himself cry at Bethany? Granted there is sorrow—but did not Christ experience sorrow at the death of his friends? But these tears, this sorrow, are tinged with the joy that Sister _____ continually preached as a Sister of _____ and as a woman of Christian hope.

Let us heed that sermon. Let us admit that joy. Let us celebrate this funeral Mass for Sister _____, bearing in mind those stirring words of St. Paul: "I have full confidence that now, as always, Christ will be exalted through me, whether I live or whether I die, for to me 'life' means Christ; hence, dying is so much gain."

CHRISTIAN MEN/AN AUTUMN EULOGY

"Honorable age is not that which stands in length of days . . . nor that which is measured by the number of years . . . having fulfilled his course on earth . . . he fulfilled long years."

These words taken from the Jewish King Solomon in the Old Testament express our sorrow at the passing of a person who needs no eulogy. His very life is the material for it and his death is the preaching of it. Such a one was _____.

It is fitting that _____ would leave us in autumn, a

beautiful time of the year when nature is at her pinnacle of perfection. Life is in the air, flowers and green grass abound. There is vibrance, vitality, buoyancy, growth, energy, and hope. This season makes us so conscious of nature. This season reminds us of life, not of death, whose boundary, as Poe says, is but a shadow and a hue. _____ would have wished it this way. How good that he did not leave us in winter when the woods are dark and the birds sing not on gloomy afternoons; he leaves us instead in this glorious time of the year when he himself would be happiest at the shore.

_____ knew well that if a man is a builder, he must be a man of thought and feeling. In his struggle to achieve great things, who would ever know the hidden battles he waged, the discouragement, the winter of discontent, the rain, the wind, the cold, the loneliness of it all. That is why the epitome of his life was the cry of Robert Browning, "I was ever a fighter—so one fight more."

Men see the surface; God sees the soul. And how clearly he must have seen this good man—the laughter in his face ready to break into merriment, the fusion of kindness and strength, the efficiency and dogged perseverence in the business arena, the charity for all. But above all the wit. It was his wit that kept him going, a wit full of old man's wisdom and young man's hopes, a profound wit that had no room for hatred and arrogance, for bigotry and prejudice.

Words are weak tools when we ask them to bear the things that can only be felt in the human heart, yet in death, _____ teaches us that love demands a fearful price from those who are touched by it. It can be bitter as well as beautiful, cutting as well as capacious. Yet love is the only hope, the only meaning.

_____ taught us love and faith. The love of _____ for people was exemplified in no better way than (give personal anecdote). Many years ago he learned that love is not love until you give it away. Sacrifice is often difficult and irksome, and only love can make it easy. Perfect love makes it a joy!

In addition to love, _____ taught us faith. Love is the cause, but the key is faith. This faith does not immunize any of us from trial and trouble, from misinterpretation and misunderstanding, from failure and falling. But this faith stands strong against the shifting winds of popular opinion and teachings. It is unbending when human events drive us to the foot of the cross! It is a faith that knows death is meaningless without Christ, for although our Church is a hard one to live in, it is a beautiful one to die in.

Today for us, there is no joyfulness, no banter, no laughter, no noise. Today there is silence, a long, reflective silence. Today we know the silence of the Creator who says:

> "I have come, _____, to gather you into my everlasting embrace so that you may have life and have it more abundantly."

To the entire _____ family, we extend our sympathy. Their loss is our loss. Their sorrow is our sorrow. There will be a little less laughter in the world. A part of all of us is gone. But I trust that _____ is with us today, for

> "He has run a good race.
> He has kept the faith.
> He has won the prize of Our Lord Jesus Christ."

A WINTER EULOGY

> "No life moves shadowless across the land, each must leave his footprint in the sand."

With these poetic words, we express our sorrow on the passing of a person who needs no eulogy. His very life is the material for it, and his death is the preaching of it. Such a man was _____.

Last _____, the curtain of his life slowly, irrevocably came down. His footprints in the sand are no more. His vocation as a father, a grandfather, a great-grandfather, a distinguished church servant, a success at his work and an extraordinary person has come to an end.

Death, when it comes, seems so often sudden. All too seldom in life do we meet a man who makes a profound and lasting impact on us. _____ was such a man. No one came within the magic of his spell without being a better person for having known him. He was a man with a master mind and a master spirit, a fusion of strength and kindness, a man with a zest for life, a thirst for truth, and a love for the outdoors, a man of business dedicated to the business of man, a person interested in the world above as well as the world below.

We celebrate his passage to eternal life. He was a builder in the real sense, a builder of people. As a man of thought and feeling, he never wrung his hands despondently. He never folded his hands complacently. He extended them generously. But, in his struggle to achieve, in his attempt to get things done, in his task of accomplishment, who would ever know the hidden battles he waged, the discouragement, the winters of discontent, the depression, the rain, the cold, the loneliness of it all!

Men see the surface, God sees the soul. And how well he must have seen _____'s sense of humor, the laughter in his face ready to break into merriment, the fusion of understanding strength, the charity for all. But, above all, the wit. It was his wit that kept him going, a wit full of old men's wisdom and young men's hopes.

Besides a sense of humor, _____ taught us faith. This faith does not immunize us from trial and trouble, from headache and heartache, from failure and falling. This faith does stand strong against the ever shifting winds of today's popular but erroneous teachings. And this faith does not bend when human events drive us to the foot of the cross.

This morning we wear white vestments because this is really a celebration of life. For death marks the beginning of a new kind of living. The seed must come to an end if the life of the flower is to begin! Today we are in the winter of the year. Trees are naked. Lawns are drab. Green hills are silent. Woods are dark. The afternoons are gloomy. Birds sing not. As the poet Emily Dickinson said of northern New England, "There is a certain slant of light . . . on a winter afternoon that oppresses like a weight . . . and shadows hold their breath on the look of death."

_____'s death cannot be blamed on heart failure, because his heart never failed him or anyone else. His heart was never a failure, but rather his greatest success. He had room in it for every joy and everyone else's joy and sorrow. Most of the time it is the heart that governs understanding, and understanding was his special quality. He not only understood human frailty, but seemed almost to prefer it.

Andre Malraux, the French Minister of Culture, once said: "I see no other light for humanity than that offered by Christianity." Each one of us has a lot of questions. Our Christian faith is the belief in a question mark. _____ would have us question in sincerity and truth. Let us remember him with questions rather than tears. His children, his dear relatives, and we, his dearest friends, will never be able to cry as much as he was able to make us laugh.

To the entire _____ family, we extend our sympathy. Their loss is our loss, their sorrow is our sorrow. There will be a little less laughter in the world; for us his gentle presence is gone. May the deep realization of his joy today counteract our profound sorrow. May we realize that his earthly dwelling is destroyed, but his eternal home is already built.

The Catholic Church has lost an apostolic layman; the community, a courageous leader; and many thousands, a sincere and self-sacrificing friend. We shall miss him but he will go on living in the monuments he has made and in the memories he has left. _____ will not have died.

He does not die who lives in the hearts of those who love him.

He does not die whose footprints remain upon the sand.

He does not die who, with St. Paul, has "run the good race, has kept the faith, and has won the prize of Our Lord, Jesus Christ."

EULOGY FOR A SPORTSMAN

> "When the One Great Scorer comes
> To write against your name—
> He marks not that you won or lost—
> But how you played the game."
>
> Grantland Rice

These are the words of a famous American sportsman, Grantland Rice. They are appropriate this day as we come to pay our last respects to a sportsman, a superfan, and for us his friends, a superstar.

We gather in a church today to show that there is another dimension and another perspective to this man. This occasion could just as easily have taken place in an auditorium, on a field, on a beach, at a cemetery, or at a funeral parlor. But we gather in a church because of our faith, hope and charity, and our rocklike conviction that we do not have here a lasting city. _____ belongs to God.

The Book of Ecclesiastes tells us, "There is an appointed time for everything." We are here this morning, my dear friends, because one of these times has come. Three days ago there came to this kind, warm-hearted man a time to die. And we, his family and friends, gather in this church to pay our homage. For us it is a time to mourn, a time to recall memories, a time to re-articulate answers to the perennial question of life and death.

Sigmund Freud said that death was the goal of all life, and Peter Pan saw it as an awfully big adventure. Socrates thought death might be the greatest of all human blessings, and contemporary theologians vie with each other to discourse learnedly on the subject of thanatology. Special ministries on death swirl all around us, and college courses explore death's individual, social, and spiritual dimensions.

Yet, amidst all this interest in death, something is missing. There is a lack, a void, an absence. Death answers the profound questions of what it means for a human being to die and what it means for a Christian to die. Thus the paradox we face today: for the deceased the pain is gone, for the survivors it lingers on; the deceased is in peace, and we the survivors anguish over a man.

A man whose passing marks another passing of a part of the heart of this great city.

A man of brilliance and memory despite little formal education.

A man who was generous to a fault to his beloved family.

A man who laughed, loved, worried, and wept; danced and dreamed, sang and served, prayed and worked.

This man is now lost to our world. This man God will not, indeed cannot, replace. This man who touched a whole unique world with his warm flame of human living is gone.

This is the reason we are sad today, and shed tears, and experience sorrow. This is a time to mourn, but, it is also, as with all human events, a time to learn. The deceased has bequeathed to us a sense of faith, of friendship, and of the fellowship of all people.

His sense of faith was tremendous. We need to be reminded frequently that nothing is impossible with God and that nothing of a life is lost, when cherished in memory, by us who love this "earthly traveler." He was forever a realist. His acute mind was uncluttered by theoretical cobwebs. He was a student of living, not of books and schools. His *summa cum laude* was of the streets. His real degree came at the end of his life, not at the beginning.

His faith in God and people was deep. He was a man of prayer who did not parade his piety. To borrow a phrase from Graham Greene, _____, as a totally amused observer of human folly, "could love men and women as God loved them," knowing the worst.

To me that is what faith is. In his last Christmas card, called "Footprints in the Sand," he gently was telling us that we are but pebbles in the sand, despite our affluence, influence, and sophistication. Love is the cause of everything, but faith is the key, and so his Judaeo-Christian religion was the bedrock of his life. If faith is an answer to a question mark, then religion is an attempt to provide a person with a meaning system, which provides answers to the most basic questions about existence.

_____ also taught us a sense of friendship. There are two lines in the poetry of Hilaire Belloc, that much underestimated poet of the Edwardian era, which strike me as especially meaningful today:

"There's nothing worth the wear of winning
But laughter and the love of friends."

The laughter and love of friends were _____'s reward on earth. The computer-like memory for stories, events, and happenings, many of which would never, or could never, be put in print, were a source of joy to all who came within his magic spell.

In the silence of death he tells us today of his high hopes. In an age troubled by crises of identity, _____ never doubted his identity. He was a Christian man dedicated to serving God and people, and not just addressing them.

In the silence of death he tells us to remember: life is a precious commodity and a perishable gift, so do not take the important things in life for granted.

In the silence of death he tells us to remember that more people are flattered into goodness than are talked out of badness.

In the silence of death he tells us to persevere day by day, with friends, as we complete our voyage back to God.

Finally, a sense of fraternity. By fraternity I mean the brotherhood of man. And just as true friendship is a plant of slow growth, _____'s friends were stretched like a gold thread around the world from every walk and station of life, black and white, rich and poor, quick and slow, courageous and fearful, public and private, extrovert and timid. In this day and age when most people have precious little room in their hearts for other people, much less God, he knew that the key word, GIVE, meant that the joy of living was the joy of giving of himself. He understood well the words of Jesus, "There is no greater love than this: to lay down one's life for one's friends."

His fraternal spirit spilled itself over through the veneer of humor exhibited in countless notes, pranks, gags, banter, and blarney. And, above all, in his wit. A wit filled with old men's wisdom and young men's hopes. A wit that had no time and no room for hatred and arrogance, bigotry and prejudice. A wit which had a humility that was able to laugh mainly at himself.

The crib of Christmas and the cross of Calvary were both made of trees. And all of us live our lives between Christmas and Easter. We can never forget Lent. The moment we are born we begin to die. There are those today who maintain that God is dead. God allows himself to be edged out of the world and onto the cross. Just as Jesus Christ, who once said, "My God, my God, why hast thou forsaken me," so too we must carry our crosses daily, and still find the courage for joy and laughter.

The late Vince Lombardi, a close friend of _____, once said, "I believe in God, and I believe in human decency. But I firmly believe that any man's finest hour—his greatest fulfillment of all he holds dear—is that moment when he has worked his heart out in a good cause and lies exhausted on the field of battle—victorious."

May the deep realization of celestial victory today counteract our profound sorrow.

May we find consolation in the awareness that he, like us, was afflicted by the certainty of death.

May we realize that his earthly dwelling is destroyed but his eternal home is ready, not a paradise lost but a paradise regained.

To the entire _____ family, we extend our sympathy. Their loss is our loss; their sorrow is our sorrow. The Catholic Church has lost an apostolic layman; the community, a courageous leader; and thousands, a sincere friend. We shall miss him, but he will go on living in the monuments he has made and in the memories he has left.

And so we bid farewell to our friend of all seasons. I am sure that he has already heard the divine accolade, "Well done, my good and faithful servant! Welcome to the reward I have prepared for you."

He does not die who lives on in the hearts of those who love him.

He does not die whose footprints remain upon the sand, for as his own card of thirteen short weeks ago read:

"One night I dreamed I was walking along the beach with the Lord, and across the sky flashed scenes from my life.

"For each scene I noticed two sets of footprints in the

sand, one belonging to me, the other to the Lord.

"When the last scene of my life flashed before me, I looked back at the footprints in the sand, and I noticed that many times along the path of my life, there was only one set of footprints in the sand.

"I also noticed that this happened at the very lowest and saddest times in my life. This bothered me, and I asked the Lord about it:

" 'Lord, you said that once I decided to follow you, you would walk with me all the way, but I have noticed that during the most troublesome times in my life, there is only one set of footprints. I don't understand why. When I needed you most, you deserted me.'

"The Lord replied, 'My precious child, I love you and I would never leave you. During your times of trial and suffering, when you saw only one set of footprints, it was then that I was carrying you.' "

CHRISTIAN WOMEN/EULOGY FOR A MOTHER

"When one finds a worthy wife, her value is far beyond pearls.
Her husband entrusts his heart to her and has an unfailing prize.
Many are the women of proven worth, but you have excelled them all."

Proverbs 31:10, 11, 29

For some persons, only the Roman orator Cicero's cynical eulogy would be fitting: "He conferred his greatest benefit on the world by his leaving it." Others, however, need no eulogy, need no acclaim, no tribute, no address, for their life is the material for the eulogy and their death is the preaching of it. Such a person was _____ .

Faith brings us together on this day, the faith that Christ urged on his apostles when he spoke these words, "Do not let your hearts be troubled. Have faith in God and faith in me." The same faith that comes to us from the apostles fills our church this morning as we assemble to bid *au revoir* to a well-loved mother, an extraordinary woman committed to the world above and the world below, a beloved friend, a respected citizen, and loyal American.

The late President John Kennedy once wrote a best-seller entitled *Profiles in Courage*, citing such notables as John Quincy Adams, Daniel Webster, and Sam Houston. Today we pay our respects to a woman who was an authentic "profile in courage" as she faced each day of her long illness.

For a practicing Christian, death leads to life. She has not died altogether, totally and utterly. She has, rather, reached the unique point of eternal life where Christ has finally taken complete and permanent possession of this kind and gentle woman. Any wonder that, with St. Paul, _____ can proclaim, "I have full confidence that now, as always, Christ will be exalted through me."

In the silence of death, _____ tells us today of her high hopes. In an age troubled by identity crises, she never doubted her basic identity. She was a Christian woman dedicated to serving God and people.

In the silence of death she tells us to remember: life is a precious commodity and a perishable gift, so do not take the important things of life for granted.

In the silence of death she tells us to persevere day by day with affection for each other, as we complete our voyage back to God to be with her.

In the silence of death she teaches us tolerance for life's refugees with human faults and foibles, for here was a woman who loved people as God loves them, knowing the worst.

In the silence of death she tells us always to keep our

promises even if we have to cross our heart, because her heart was her greatest success. It was always giving, never taking. She knew full well that "people who need people are the luckiest people in the world."

Jesus once said, "In my father's house are many mansions." Paradoxically we can say today with E.E. Cummings, "In our mother's heart there were many songs, in her mind was an abyss of light, in her soul there were rooms of love."

Her love was so often shown with her hands—small, slender, sturdy, moving with the precision of a machine. Hands that were forever cooking, scrubbing, nursing, sewing, dusting, teaching, and giving to others. They were also adept at holding the hands of her children.

Her love was her _____-year existence in this city, her early education, her nursing career, her marriage, her Church, her tireless sacrifices of her time and talents for others that ultimately won for her the coveted accolade, "Nurse of the Year," given by her college alumni association.

Her love was the *fiat* of another Mary, who said "Be it done unto me." Her love was the *fiat* of acceptance, of resignation, and of submission.

The laughter and the love of myriad friends were _____'s reward on earth. For here was a woman of compassion, strength, sanity, and common sense, a woman who laughed, loved, worried, and wept; danced and dreamed, sang and served, prayed and worked.

Words are weak tools when we ask them to bare the feelings of the heart. Our words are to the entire _____ family and to countless friends as we extend our sympathy. It is a time to mourn, to recall memories, and to re-articulate answers.

Our lives, so variously touched by hers, have lost a dimension. Some measure of our human experience has been withdrawn. Because this will not grow less with time, we have no provision for sorrow.

Granted there is grief today, but was not Christ edged off this earth onto a cross and did he not say, "My God, my God, why have you forsaken me?"

Granted there are tears today, but did not Jesus cry at Bethany?

Granted there is sorrow, but did not Christ weep at the death of his friend, Lazarus?

Because we are her family and her friends, we miss her.

It is time to mourn. But because we are Christians, because we believe, it is also a time for us to rejoice that _____ is happy and at peace at last.

Through this marvelous woman Christ was very much exalted and, indeed, as St. Paul said, "There is, therefore, no condemnation for those who die"—as _____ died—very, very much, "in Christ Jesus."

May she rest forever in peace, joy and happiness!

CHRISTIAN YOUTH/EULOGY FOR A YOUNG MAN

Across the ages we hear many a cry of grief at the premature extinction of the young. "The beauty of Israel lies pierced on the high place," sang David of his young comrade Jonathan, slain on Mt. Gilboa. Lycidias was mourned by his boyhood friend Milton who said, "Lycidias hath not left a peer." Tragedy is the difference between what is and what might have been, but neither the Jewish warrior nor Milton's friend was cut off at the height of such promise as the young man so quickly snatched from us last Friday.

There was a young man, who knew when to speak and when to act.

There was a young man, who knew the difference between patience and hesitation.

There was a young man who knew well the price of failure and the reward of success.

There was your young friend, who cared and shared at all times.

There was a young man, with common sense beyond his years.

Yes, there came a man, a good and honest man, a young man; his name was _____. And in a moment he was no more.

Today death is an enemy. It suggests the memorable words of the Roman poet, Virgil: "O pale death, you come to the huts of the poor as well as the palaces of the kings." Today we wear white vestments that in the Church symbolize _____'s new life. Today the Church sprinkles holy water to show this is the celebration of the living. For the Christian death marks the beginning of a new kind of living.

In 1870 Nietzsche, the German philosopher, said, "He who has a 'why' can put up with any 'how.'" This is where our Christian way of life comes in. Religion is an attempt to provide us with a meaning system, giving answers to the most basic questions about our existence. Without the "why" we can never accept the "how."

It is in the winter of the year that the most dynamic words of Sacred Scripture come to pass, the explosive words of St. John, "The Word was made flesh and came to dwell among us." God entered our history, and this brings to every thinking person a mood of vibrance, vitality, energy, and hope—a reminder not of death but of life, both here and hereafter. For the life of the seed must come to an end if the life of the flower is to begin.

And what a life has just begun for _____! St. Paul tells us, "Eye has not seen . . . what God has prepared for those who love him." As T.S. Eliot, speaking of the Christian, said, "Our plea is not for Paradise lost but an epic of Paradise regained."

Pericles, the great Greek orator, when asked to memorialize fallen Greek war heroes, said that no words should be spoken, but that their lives should be woven into the stuff of other men's lives that follow. So be it.

The deceased accomplished much in his short years. To the _____ family we extend our love. To his countless friends we extend our sympathy. Their sorrow and loss are ours. But for all of us life goes on. Although the brightness has faded from the air, the world continues in the same orbit, but it is a somewhat different world.

Each one of us must reflect on this young man, on his wit and wisdom, on his cool mind and warm heart.

Each one of us must complete the voyage he began so well.

And so we bid *au revoir* to our young man and our young friend of all seasons. I am sure that _____ has already heard the divine accolade, "Well done, my good and faithful servant! Welcome to the reward I have prepared for you."

On the mount of the resplendent Transfiguration, the impulsive Peter said, "It is good for us to be here." Today we say, "It was good for us to have been with him."

Yes, tragedy is the difference between what is and what might have been. May _____ rest in peace and happiness.

EULOGY FOR A CHILD

"The bruised reed shall not be broken."

Isaiah 42:3

Today not one of us would be here at _____ if we had a choice about the life and death of others. Yet each one of us is here today because we are a people who believe earnestly the meaning of the words of the prophet, Isaiah, who says to us,

"The bruised reed shall not be broken." For, indeed, the reed that has been bruised has not been broken; it has been given the life that all of us seek, the life that is everlasting.

Today our hearts are hurting, and will for days to come. The wound that creates our pain will not easily be healed. And yet, I say that the little boy we have given to God is at this moment with the Lord Jesus in glory among all his saints. His is from this day on the peace and the abounding joy of being with our heavenly Father, the God who made him.

And why? There has been no word uttered more painfully, more pleadingly, and more frequently. Why? Why did God ask of us a gift so precious? Why? Why at this time?

Only God can answer. And today he is sharing with this boy the meaning of his will for all of us.

_____ and _____, and their families, friends, and all of us who love _____ must look out beyond our human experience to the Lord Jesus. We must look through the life, as short as it was, of a little boy who is beyond doubt an image of Jesus. For to say that _____ loved those who were close to him is not enough. He loved them tenderly and with all his heart even in his suffering. For us to wonder whether courage is a part of childhood is senseless. All of us together have not enough courage to equal the calm, heroic bravery that marked the last eight weeks of _____'s life. And again not unlike Jesus, _____ has done in his life what Jesus did in his life—he has brought us, even in our severe sorrow and utter helplessness, to the Father. Even though _____ was not fully aware of all that faith and religion are for us, he is like St. Paul who wrote to his friends, "That illness gave me the opportunity to preach the Good News of Jesus Christ to you."

We must continue our lives now. And we must do so with the same spirit of bravery that we have been privileged to witness these last five years and most specially these last few weeks of _____'s life.

Yes, our lives are changed—and radically so. Nevertheless, we must continue to pray, no longer for _____, but for one another. For we have given a gift to God, a gift who is spotless, an immaculate offering who today stands in glory with all the saints in heaven. We must pray that the Lord Jesus and his Mother, Mary, will specially intercede for us before God the Father that we may never lose sight of the special love God has asked of us at this moment in our lives.

Yes, we prayed. Our petitions were united with those of friends and others who knew _____ only by name. And God answered our prayers in a way that is beyond our comprehension. We prayed for renewed health and human life. God gave us a new life, a new saint who now lives among the elect with God.

And so our prayers are also prayers of gratitude, for we must thank God that we have loved and lived with a saint of God.

What Isaiah says to us is so true: "The bruised reed shall not be broken." For the life that was human and bruised has not been broken. _____ has risen to the glory and perfection of everlasting life with God, Creator of all life.

IMMORTALITY

Do not stand at my grave and weep.
I am not there. I do not sleep.

I am a thousand winds that blow.
I am the diamond glints on snow.
I am the sunlight on ripened grain.
I am the gentle autumn rain.
When you awake in the morning's hush,
I am the swift unflinging rush
Of quiet birds in circling flight.

I am the soft star shine at night.
Do not stand at my grave and cry.
I am not there. I did not die.

Author Unknown

ANNIVERSARIES

SERMON FOR A SILVER ANNIVERSARY
OF PRIESTHOOD

"Taking Peter, James, and John, Jesus went up to a high mountain, called Thabor. Suddenly, he was transfigured before their eyes—his face shining like the sun, his garments becoming white as snow. And seeing this, Peter called out: 'Lord, it is good for us to be here!'"

Matthew 17:1, 2, 4

A psychologist recently remarked that life involves three major choices: a mate, a mission, and a master. His thinking is that every man, at one time or another, must choose a mate, someone to love. Also a mission, something to do. And finally a master, someone to follow.

If such a thesis be psychologically sound, then today's celebration is a powerful corollary. For what are we doing this morning but paying tribute to the triple choice adopted by our jubilarian twenty-five years ago? What else but hailing the trinity of choices irrevocably pronounced in a small church in his native city by the young deacon? What else but joyfully recalling those historic choices of _____ by which he dramatically selected Jesus as his partner, the priesthood as his mission, and the Catholic Church as his master? Looking back upon a quarter-century of perseverance in these choices, is it any wonder that like St. Peter, we too this morning cry out: "Lord, it is good for us to be here!"

Good? Paradoxically a growing number of Catholics today would disagree. An increasing array of Church critics would vehemently question the wisdom behind our jubilarian's triple choice of twenty-five years ago. "This is the age of Vatican II," these people remind us. "The age of ag-giornamento. The age of the priesthood of the faithful. The day is coming when the priest will be hardly distinguishable from the layman. He will wear secular clothes—and they will no longer be black. He will sport a fancy tie, not the old-fashioned Roman collar. And, of course, he will be married, not celibate. The day is coming when the more highly educated Catholics will not seek guidance from the priest. After all, sacramental powers do not imply charismatic wisdom in solving the problems of life. We have psychiatrists to consult in matters of personality adjustment. We have competent lay educators to handle the training of our children. We have sociologists to guide our thinking on civic and community problems. To put it bluntly, the priesthood is out of touch with our changing post-Vatican II world. In fact, in today's updated Church, the priesthood is an outdated anachronism!"

Such a point of view is, of course, extreme. But in this age of religious sensationalism and Christian ferment, it is being more and more encountered. Hence, a few words in defense of the ministerial priesthood might this morning be in order. After all, sixteen hundred years ago St. Augustine remarked that "In this life, there is nothing more difficult—or more beautiful—than the office of a priest." And as we join with Father _____ in celebrating twenty-five years of his priestly office, let us pose the identical question every sacerdotal jubilarian asks as he celebrates his anniversary Mass: "What is the priesthood? What justifies its existence? What does it mean to be a priest?"

What does it mean? Being a priest means all the hours our jubilarian spends between early Mass in the morning and going to bed late at night. It means the instructions, the confessions, the religion classes, the counseling. It means the wife whose husband gambles, and the husband nagged by his wife.

The adolescent whose parents are old-fashioned, and the parents whose children are modern adolescents. The people who want no more children, and those who want them but cannot have them. It means the scientific agnostic who believes nothing, and the lady who says she has visions, and believes everything. The little girl who wants her rosary blessed, the couple who want their marriage blessed.

What is the priesthood? It is the happiness our jubilarian feels every time he pours the Christianizing waters of baptism over the head of a loudly complaining baby, and the sadness he feels as he lays to rest one of the sheep of his fold. It is the discouragement coming from the realization that his words from the pulpit and his advice in the confessional are heeded so little, and the thrill that shakes his soul when he hears, "Father, it has been twenty years since my last confession." It is his sense of contact with the good when he gives First Communion to the innocent, and it is the terror of the powers of evil when a soul leaves the confessional unabsolved. It is the feeling of genuine satisfaction that rises from the good convert, and it is the guilty feeling of anxiety aroused by the fallen away Catholic.

What is the priesthood? It is the good feeling that comes from preparing a dying Christian to meet his Maker, and the sorrow that comes from having been called too late to the deathbed of a lapsed Catholic. It is the happiness that comes from celebrating the Nuptial Mass for the bride and groom he has known since they were children, and the loneliness that comes occasionally on Christmas and Easter when he realizes that although he belongs to all families, he is really a member of none.

What is the priesthood? It is liturgical planning committees, and CCD meetings, and parish renewal. It is the unending chain of meetings on budgets, on child care, on the aged, and on the sick. It means raising money, running bazaars, announcing second collections. It means building and supervision; maintenance and expansion; the breviary said late at night; and the rosary said in snatches throughout the day.

What is the priesthood? It is the Pontifical Mass, the Concelebrated Mass, and thirty minutes each day completely alone with God. It is the priest silhouetted against the headlights of a police car, as he anoints an accident victim. It is a chaplain in the armed forces moving along the front lines conferring the last rites and murmuring words of encouragement, when his own soul is sick with fear. It is the old priest saying the stations of the cross in the light of the sanctuary lamp in the monastery chapel. It is the young seminarian filled with zeal and longing for the day when he shall achieve his goal.

What is the priesthood? It is all these things and more. And when we consider twenty-five glorious years during which these services were generously offered to countless people, we truly have a reason for rejoicing with Father _____. For if we are correct in asserting that Vatican II emphasizes that today's priest must be a man of service, if we are correct in stating that this magnificent Council directs its pastors to reach beyond their own "flock" and become involved with those sheep outside their fold, if we are correct in interpreting the true spirit of aggiornamento to be a call not just for new liturgy, the lay apostolate, and social involvement, but also for vitally functioning priests, clerics very much "about their Father's business," then looking at this man who has labored all his priestly life in parishes, high schools, and seminaries here and abroad, looking at this man who during his five years on Staten Island has become much involved with the whole ecumenical movement, looking at this man who has embodied for the past quarter-century the spirit of our recent Council, we can truly say with Peter: "Lord, it is good for us to be here."

Good for Father _____'s mother and brother, for instance. They are also celebrating this anniversary today at the
_____'s family home in _____. Father _____'s father
never received his son's first priestly blessing. He died shortly
before ordination. But his mother did, and today I am sure she
is reliving that moment. That moment in which she took the
newly anointed hands of her priest-son and pressed them to
her lips. Hands that she had washed when _____ was a boy.
Hands that she had at times rapped. Hands that she had
undoubtedly bandaged. Hands that for twenty-five years have
remained consecrated to Jesus Christ. Yes, Lord, it is good for
the _____ family to be here in spirit today. How does the
poet put it?

> We need them in life's early morning, we need them again
> at its close;
> We feel their warm clasp of true friendship, we seek them
> when tasting life's woes.
> When we come to this world we are sinful, the greatest as
> well as the least.
> And the hand that makes us pure as angels is the beautiful
> hand of the priest.
> At the altar each day we behold them and the hands of a
> king on his throne
> Are not equal to them in their greatness, their dignity
> stands all alone;
> For there in the stillness of morning, ere the sun has
> emerged from the East,
> There God rests between the pure fingers of the beautiful
> hands of a priest.
> And when we are tempted and wander to pathways of
> shame and of sin,
> 'Tis the hand of a priest will absolve us—not once, but
> again and again;

And when we are taking life's partner, other hands may
prepare us a feast,
But the hand that will bless and unite us is the beautiful
hand of a priest.
God bless them and keep them all holy for the Host which
their fingers caress;
What can a poor sinner do better than to ask Him, Who
choose thee to bless?
When the death-dews on our eyelids are falling, may our
courage and strength be increased,
By seeing raised o'er us in blessing the beautiful hand of a
priest!

This summer, _____ will once again kiss these hands.
"Lord, it is good for us to be here!"

It is good finally for the friends, relatives and parishioners
of our jubilarian. Beyond any doubt, this era of renewal has
been a difficult time for us Christians. Vatican II has pulled the
cork from a bottle, and many of us have all but been drowned.
New changes, new ideas, and new structures have sprung up
on every side. So much is being said about our changing role,
our 20th-century ministry, and our modern-day vocation. Yet
Karl Rahner, the eminent German theologian, has put this
confusion to rest with a brilliant, insightful perspective: "Man
does not have a vocation," Rahner says. "He is a vocation!"
Hence man's real value comes, not from his function, but from
his personhood. Not from his role, but from his identity. Not
from what he does, but from who he is.

You and I are here today because of who our jubilarian is.
For _____ is a leader. A leader in the liturgical celebration of
the Eucharist and other sacraments. A leader in ecumenical
involvement and social concern. A leader interested not only in
delivering Christ's message, but in shaping his image.

Sigmund Dragastin, a noted priest-psychologist, has very

profoundly described today's priest as "the expressive leader" of the Christian community. According to Father Dragastin, there is a distinct difference between being an "instrumental" leader and being an "expressive" leader. An instrumental leader is one whose primary concern is getting things done. The fulfillment of tasks, organization, administration, and implementation are important to him. He is a doer, a planner, a decision-maker. The expressive leader, on the other hand, is more concerned about vision, morale, and philosophy. He soothes hurt feelings, reassures the troubled, encourages the weary, makes peace between the angry, and inspires the discouraged. The instrumental leader, then, answers questions. The expressive leader asks them. The instrumental leader tells people what to do; the expressive leader challenges them to do their best. The instrumental leader lays down the law; the expressive leader stirs up the heart. In fine, the instrumental leader is a man who does. The expressive leader is a man who is.

Father _____ is an expressive leader, because of who he is. Because of who he has been for these past twenty-five years, you and I can truly say with Peter: "Lord, it is good for us to be here!"

And so, be we related to our jubilarian by family ties, by priestly profession, or by parochial friendship, all of us here in _____ Church are happy to be present at this celebration. Thank you for inviting us, Father _____. Congratulations on that triple choice you made twenty-five years ago when you chose Jesus Christ as your mate, the Catholic Church as your master, and the ministerial priesthood as your mission. "Lord, it is good for us to be here!"

SERMON FOR A GOLDEN JUBILEE/RELIGIOUS

"Lord, it is good for us to be here. If you will, let us set up three tabernacles—one for you, one for Moses, and one for Elias."

Matthew 17:4

Time loved it. The *Washington Post* panned it. Many critics said it was all the things movies aren't supposed to be any more. But it broke attendance records for weeks in movie houses across the country. I am speaking, of course, of the film, *Love Story.*

Starring Ali McGraw and Ryan O'Neal, *Love Story* heralded a new kind of romanticism that has beyond doubt characterized life in the United States for these past several years. But it did something else too. It preached a masterful sermon about today's Church and our place in it. Recall, for instance, the scene in which Barrett notices a medal around Jenny's neck. He asks, "Why did you leave it?" "Leave what?" replies Jenny. "The Church," is the response. "Oh, the Church," Jenny says, "I didn't leave it; I just never joined it!"

"I just never joined it!" You and I are here today, my dear friends, to witness a real-life sequel to that startling statement in Eric Segal's *Love Story.* We are here today to honor two Sisters who fifty years ago joined the Church in a unique way. We are here today to share in the golden jubilee celebration of Sister _____ and Sister _____, two women who for the last half century have produced, directed, and lived their own *Love Story.*

First, during the last fifty years, Sister _____ and Sister _____ have produced their own *Love Story.* We call this act of production a vocation to the religious life, fidelity to God's call, a commitment to permanency.

Permanency! Perhaps it is to this particular area that our golden jubilarians really speak today. In an age stressing transience over permanency, in an age characterized by a Kleenex mentality, the throwing away of things and relationships, in an age of soaring divorces, trial marriages, and high turnover both at home and at work, the permanency of these Sisters' commitment as religious women shines forth.

Isn't it true? Young Sisters today are asking some penetrating questions about permanent commitment. Can I really pledge a lifelong fidelity to religious life? How can I commit myself to this Institute forever, irrevocably, irretrievably? Older Sisters are asking the same basic question. "So much has changed since I entered this order. Is it the same congregation to which I vowed myself permanently?" Today's golden jubilee can pour soothing oil on such troubled waters. For in Sister _____ and Sister _____, we see two women who have made a commitment, not to an institute, not to a sense of community, not to a quest for holiness, but rather to Jesus Christ.

When people talk of commitment today, they are generally talking about one of three kinds of commitment. The first might be called an institutionalized commitment.

Some live out their religious life as basically a devotion to their institute. They identify themselves with the structures and traditions of the community and with the institutions it has built up. They take a basic pride in belonging to this particular religious institute and devote their energies to improving its function, prestige, and influence in society.

Other religious see their commitment as centered on people rather than on what is institutional. They say they entered the religious life to find Christian community. Their interpretation accentuates the idea of primary, face-to-face relationships. It puts its finger on an aspect of religious life that is real, human, and true. It recognizes that the community is the soul of the institute and is what makes the institute a coherent and stable historical reality. Despite the most radical institutional changes, the institute is really made up of its personnel. This interpretation sees that the community is a more important human reality than the institute with all its organized apostolates which identify the members with the institutions.

A third way of looking at the commitment of the religious life is that of a quest for salvation, or an attaining of Christian perfection. In this interpretation, one enters the religious life because of the ideal of the Christian life it represents. The vows are seen as a commitment to become a good religious and to realize in oneself a deep life of prayer and a fruitful service to God's people.

The difficulty with these three commitments is that each lacks theological insight. Suppose I made my commitment to an institute. Look at what has happened—so much has changed. Can this any longer be called the same community I entered? One could then question the continuance of the commitment of the vows by arguing that their object hardly exists any longer. Everything has changed—the garb, the rule, the customs, the works. So then how can one be held in God's sight to vows made to something which has changed so much as no longer to be the same?

Other kinds of temptations to leave are likely to come to those committed to personal community. What if our friends have left, or we simply fail to find the warmth and virtue of true Christian community in the congregation? What if we find much truer community with friends outside? If our commitment of the vows is basically motivated by the quest for community, then if we come to feel that community is very inadequate in our own institute, we will be strongly inclined to leave and to seek fellowship where it is experienced as much more alive.

Even the specifically religious interpretation contains occasions for the temptation to leave. What if we find that we have not become good religious, that the religious form of life has not led us to an intense prayer life or a successful apostolate? What if we feel ourselves dying on the vine, where the test of years shows we have not realized in our lives the ideal we were seeking by taking vows? If this way of life has not brought us to the deep union with God we were expecting, we may be tempted to leave.

Our golden jubilarians show us the secret of permanent commitment. For fifty years they have been committed not to things but to a person. Not to an institution, sense of community, or quest for sanctity, but to Jesus Christ. Here is the answer to our permanent commitment—being anchored in the person of Jesus, producing a *Love Story* in the company of Christ himself.

Second, during the last fifty years, Sister _____ and Sister _____ have directed their own *Love Story*, a direction concretized, actualized, and manifested by their vows.

By their vow of poverty, our golden jubilarians have publicly proclaimed things are a means, not an end. For them, in the words of Vatican II, things are to be gratuitously shared to further the kingdom of God. For them, the materialism of a world entranced with higher salaries, more and more possessions, and bigger houses is poignantly challenged.

By the vow of chastity, our golden jubilarians have publicly proclaimed a total sexual commitment to the kingdom of Jesus. An unlimited womanly love for all God's people. A gauntlet hurled at the world.

By their vow of obedience, our golden jubilarians have publicly proclaimed not a giving up of individuality, personhood, or independence; rather, a giving out of whatever talents are demanded for God's kingdom. In a world in which people are used and exploited, obedience teaches how people can be loved and cherished.

Hence the *Love Story* of our golden jubilarians assumes its direction—No fuss—just love.

Someone has said that it takes three people to make a

successful marriage. A girl and her anxious parents! If this be true, then we must look at the third element of today's golden jubilee celebration.

During the last fifty years, Sister ___ ___ and Sister _____ have lived their own *Love Story*, within the community of the _____.

This is the reason our jubilarians can live their *Love Story*. As Sisters of _____, they have never neglected that most basic prayer of human beings, the prayer of laughter, joy, and happiness, the prayer that salutes the basic goodness of this world, the prayer that responds to God's graciousness in giving us the gift of life.

May this spirit of joyful living continue for many, many years. May you Sisters of _____ continue, like our jubilarians, to be modern without being trendy; committed without being shrill; feminists but still feminine; open to new ideas yet skeptical of magical answers; very much part of your own era, yet eschatological witnesses of God's kingdom. In short, live your *Love Story* like Sister _____ and Sister _____ have for the last half century.

"Lord, it is good for us to be here!" As I conclude, I am reminded of an incident that occurred during a recent pilgrimage to the Holy Land. Israel is a living, throbbing, pulsing nation. I spent a month wandering throughout this exciting land, some of it much the way it must have been in the time of Jesus.

This is particularly true of the region called Galilee. Yet it was in Galilee that I came upon a puzzling situation. There are two famous adjacent seas in Palestine. One is fresh, and fish live in it. Splashes of green adorn its banks. Trees spread their branches over it. Along the shores of this lake children play today, as children played when Jesus was there. For Jesus loved this first lake. He could look across its silver surface when he preached his parables. On a rolling plain not far away he fed five thousand people. The River Jordan fashions this sea with sparkling water from the hills. Men build their houses near it, and birds their nests. Every kind of life is happier because this sea is here. It is the Sea of Galilee.

Lying south of the Sea of Galilee is the second sea. It too is fashioned by the flow of the River Jordan. But here things are different. There is no splash of fish, no fluttering leaf, no song of birds, no children's laughter. Here the traveler seldom passes, and the air hangs heavy. Here neither man, nor beast, nor fowl stops to drink. For this sea is full of salt, decay and stagnation. It is the Dead Sea.

The Sea of Galilee. The Sea of the Dead. What causes the mighty difference between these two neighboring bodies of water? Not the River Jordan, for this river empties the same good water into both. Not the soil in which the seas lie, for it is the same. Not the country or climate round about, for both lie in Palestine.

What is the difference? Only this. The Sea of Galilee receives but does not keep the Jordan. For every drop that flows into this sea, another drop flows out—flows out to the second connecting sea. But the second sea is shrewder, hoarding its income jealously. It will not be tempted into any generous impulse. Every drop it gets, it keeps. The Sea of Galilee thus gives and lives. The second sea gives nothing. Hence, it is named the Dead. This is the story behind the two seas in Palestine.

The meaning is obvious. There are two kinds of *Love Story* today. The first, which is selfish, self-seeking, and uncommitted, is the celluloid version of phony people who don't join the Church. The second, which is generous, committed to Christ, and joyful, is the real-life version exemplified by our golden jubilarians.

One poet puts it this way:

"What is true love, pray tell?
Love that itself forgets.
When is true love deepest?
When love more love begets.
When is true love richest?
When for naught else it leaves.
What is true love's language?
Love does not speak—it gives."

It gives as our golden jubilarians have for the last half century. Think back to the film of Eric Segal's *Love Story*. And then think of the real-life version we celebrate today in this chapel. Truly, this is a *Love Story*. Produced for Jesus Christ. Directed by the religious vows. Lived by Sister _____ and Sister _____ as joyful Sisters of the _____, their glorious religious congregation.

SERMON FOR A GOLDEN MARRIAGE JUBILEE

In 1973 the Public Broadcasting Service presented a series of life portraits of a family in Santa Barbara, California. This series, produced under the name of *An American Family*, offered an honest and candid portrayal of the day-to-day life of Mr. and Mrs. Loud and their five children. The film was made with the full permission and knowledge of all the family members.

By the time the series had ended, however, many viewers were shocked. The revelations of this American family included not just the usual fights and tensions of familial living, but the torn arena of minds and souls and the divorce of the parents. On the last show of the series, the Loud's eighteen year old son summed up what many viewers instinctively sensed. "What you have been seeing," he said, "are seven lonely people trying desperately to love each other—and not succeeding!"

Today we are celebrating just the opposite. Not a televised family of seven that shocks us, but a real life family of _____ that inspires us. Not a husband and wife preparing for a divorce, but a husband and wife preparing to reaffirm their marriage vows of fifty years ago. Not a commentary on what Kate Millet calls "The Marriage Trap," but a witnessing to what Jesus calls Christian love between a husband and wife. I am speaking, of course, of today's golden jubilee celebration of the marriage of Mr. and Mrs. _____.

The importance of today's celebration is extraordinary. Its value for you and for me is breathtaking. What we are witnessing today is a refreshing note of confidence in the traditional wedding ring. In an age when couples are complaining that their marriages have neither the sweetness of a coffee ring nor the fun of a circus ring, you and I need to be reassured that Christian marriage is not a loose-leaf ring!

You and I are familiar with the many present-day attacks on marriage. But the attacks are not only coming from feminists and from selfish playboys. In our society we now see an escalating divorce rate, undercutting one out of every three marriages. We see the institution of marriage assailed by the young who simply move in together and eschew the traditional and binding marriage vows. We see the rise of communal living where children are raised in common and couples cannot be identified as belonging to each other at all. We turn on television talk shows and see married men and women discussing mate-swapping and bisexuality. And, of course, we observe that if the contraceptive fails, murder, euphemistically called abortion, will solve the inconvenient pregnancy.

Yes, the attacks on marriage seem to be everywhere. It would appear that marriage is in trouble. But is it really? Are the signs of the times really pointing to the erosion of marriage and its future death? Is it only frightened, "unliberated" people who will continue to get married? As Christians, are we simply kidding ourselves in trying to hold on to something called "Christian marriage"?

Looking at _____ and _____ today, we are certain the answer is no. Christian marriage is as alive and well today as it was fifty years ago. It has not and will not die.

Think of it this way. A Christian is a person who follows Jesus. Jesus has said, "This is my commandment: that you love one another as I have loved you." The definition of a Christian then is one who responds to and lives God's love. The Church is Jesus in that it shows people what God's love is and how to respond to it.

The Biblical story of the prophet Hosea underscores this thesis. Hosea lived and prophesied in the latter half of the eighth century before Christ, during the period when the Northern Kingdom fell to the Assyrians and the ten "lost tribes" were deported. He predicted the disaster. But his poetic oracles also spoke of possible salvation, if only the people would turn away from foreign gods, from the cults of Baal, which flourished in Israel.

Apparently Hosea was a simple man, a farmer turned prophet during his struggle with an agonizing personal problem. The problem was his wife, Gomer. After she and Hosea were married and had had two children, something went terribly wrong. Gomer was unfaithful many times, and Hosea finally pronounced the formula of divorce. Gomer then became a sacred prostitute in one of the sanctuaries of Baal.

In the tragedy of his own life, Hosea saw a symbol of the tragedy experienced by Yahweh in his dealings with the people of Israel. Yahweh chose Israel as a man chooses a bride, but the nation prostituted itself by running after other lovers, other gods.

But among Hosea's dire predictions there sounds another, more hopeful note.

"She will run after lovers, but not overtake them,
    she will seek them, but not find them.
Then she will say, 'I shall go back to my first
    husband, for it was better with me then than now.'
Therefore, behold I shall allure her,
    I shall bring her into the desert and speak
    to her heart.
There she will respond as in the days of her youth,
    as in the days when she went up from the land
    of Egypt."

This story of Hosea and Gomer in the Old Testament is a graphic illustration of Christian marriage. Note the intimacy that the Biblical author uses to describe the relationship, not only of man and wife, but also of God and his chosen people. The Biblical author does not hesitate to use sexual imagery to present a God who is intensely involved with his people. Did not St. Paul speak of the Church as the bride of Christ? Hence the relationship between Hosea and Gomer is a sign of God's love for his Christian people of the New Testament, a sign of Christ's relationship with his Church of today.

For fifty years _____ and _____ have been signs of God's love. They have been signs through their vocation as married Christians. It is this sign-making activity that we especially honor this afternoon.

Perhaps at no time in Christian history has the need been greater for the witness of Christian marriages. As so many of our contemporaries flounder about in a sexual and marital wilderness, fearful of the future, distrusting themselves and the other sex, hearkening to the latest prophets of marital doom, we have need for more marriages like the one of _____ and _____ whose golden jubilee we celebrate this afternoon. Thank you for inviting us, _____ and _____.

Our warmest congratulations. I know I speak for all present in
saying, despite the series on PBS, "*You* are our American
Family."

SERMON AT A RELIGIOUS PROFESSION

"Then Peter addressed Jesus saying, 'Lord, it is good for
us to be here. If you will, let us set up three tents here, one
for you, one for Moses, and one for Elias.'"

Matthew 17:4

"To dream the impossible dream,
To fight the unbeatable foe,
To bear with unbearable sorrow,
To run where the brave dare not go.
This is my quest, to follow that star,
No matter how hopeless, no matter how far."

These familiar lyrics are from "The Impossible Dream,"
the hit song from the popular musical, *Man of La Mancha*. In
this show, the fabled Don Quixote comes alive. He is a laughable knight errant, a crazy charlatan fighting windmills, a silly
comic scorned for championing outmoded valor. Yet, by the
end of the play, Quixote's way of life is vindicated. At his
deathbed, those who had heeded this man's philosophy are
dramatically converted. The soiled scullery maid becomes a
lady. The stuttering friar becomes an articulate ecclesiastic.
The simple Sancho becomes a lordly noble. The final scene
sees our hero and his compatriots lustily singing those memorable lines, "To dream the impossible dream!"
    Our presence here this morning is an eloquent affirma-
tion of Don Quixote's wisdom in dreaming the impossible
dream. After all, here we are—men and women, religious and
laity, relatives and friends—gathered together to celebrate the

profession of novices, to rejoice with these men who today uniquely commit themselves to the one Church of Christ, and to share in the happiness of _____ people of God who this morning dramatically reaffirm their baptismal vows through the taking of their religious vows. Truly, "it is good for us to be here."

Or is it? Critics hasten to assure us that in this very celebration we dream an impossible dream, that this very rejoicing with our novices is following a star that is both hopeless and far. From the porticoes of St. Peter's to the pamphlet racks of St. Patrick's, people are asking, "Does the religious life have a future? Is it really relevant? It may have been in the past, but what about now?"

Some theologians intensely believe that communal worship is the Holy Spirit's message to the contemporary church—so doesn't this make a life in which private prayer is encouraged a wasteful delusion? Other theologians insist that the person, the individual, is the supreme value of today—so isn't a religious order, then, with its stress on community, something *passé*? Still other critics accent marriage as the fullest sacramental expression of manhood—so doesn't this make the vow of celibacy about to be professed this morning really an anomaly?

Because collegiality is good, obedience is bad. Because short term commitment is in, lifelong permanency, like vows, is out. As the median age of men and women in the world goes down, the median age of those in religious life goes up. So how can today's celebration be anything but an impossible dream? With the religious life so irrelevant, aren't these novices following a star that is both hopeless and far?

Such rhetorical questions might seem extreme. Yet in this age of religious sensationalism and Christian ferment, they are being frequently asked. Hence, let me say something in favor of the religious life. All too often we hear about what's wrong; let me this morning speak up for what's right. After all, someone once remarked that it takes two people to make a marriage—a girl and her anxious mother. So too does it take two sides to realistically picture today's religious life. And as we join with these _____ men in celebrating their religious profession, let us ask these essential questions: "What is the religious life? What justifies its existence? Is it really a possible dream?"

For me, the religious life is basically a life of protest. I use the word, *protest*, in its strict etymological sense; to "protest," says Webster, means to "publicly declare." And what does the religious life publicly declare? It speaks the Gospel message of Jesus Christ. It is a public declaration to society of the proper Christian attitudes towards things, people and sex. Toward things, by the vow of poverty. Toward people, by the vow of obedience. Toward sex, by the vow of celibacy. And it is precisely this public declaration that makes the religious life an effective protest. It is the open nature of the vows shortly to be pronounced this morning that makes the religious life relevant. By this public ceremony, these _____ men effectively present to society the message of Jesus Christ about things, people and sex.

The religious life will only be relevant as long as society needs to hear the message of Jesus. Does society today need this message? Look at its attitude towards things. Has the world become over-materialized? Are things a means or an end? Does what you possess become the measure of who you are? Look at society's attitude towards people. Are people loved and cherished today? Or in this age of depersonalization, are they often used and exploited? Have things become the measure of people? Look at society's attitude towards sex. Is sex equated with love? Can a person love fully and at the same time voluntarily abstain from sexual activity?

The answer is obvious. The religious life is one way of taking these three values taught by Jesus and publicly presenting them to society. Members openly profess that people are more important than things by poverty, that people are to be cherished and served by obedience, and that people can be loved in an unlimited but not necessarily sexual way by celibacy. As long as society needs this public presentation of the Gospel message, the religious life will be relevant. When society attains the truly Christian outlook on things, people, and sex, then will the religious life lose its necessity. But theologians tell us we will then have reached the messianic kingdom. It will then be the parousia.

This is what gives the religious life a future. This is what makes our profession this morning a possible dream. These young men are effectively proclaiming the message of Jesus. "Lord, it is good for us to be here!"

About this time last year, I was fortunate enough to be leading a pilgrimage to the Holy Land. It was an awesome and thrilling experience. Israel is a living, throbbing, pulsing nation. I spent a month wandering throughout this exciting land, some of it much the way it must have been in the time of Jesus.

This is particularly true of the region called Galilee. Yet it was in Galilee that I came upon a puzzling situation. There are two famous adjacent seas in Palestine. One is fresh and fish live in it. Splashes of green adorn its banks. Trees spread their branches over it. Along the shores of this lake children play today, as children played when Jesus was there. For Jesus loved this first lake. He could look across its silver surface when he preached his parables. On a rolling plain not far away he fed five thousand people. The River Jordan fashions this sea with sparkling water from the hills. Men build their houses near to it, and birds their nests. Every kind of life is happier because this sea is here. It is the Sea of Galilee.

Lying south of the Sea of Galilee is the second sea. It too is fashioned by the flow of the River Jordan. But here things are different. Here there is no splash of fish, no fluttering leaf, no song of birds, no children's laughter. Here the traveler seldom passes, and the air hangs heavy. Here neither man, nor beast, nor fowl stops to drink. For this sea is full of salt, decay, and stagnation. It is the Dead Sea.

The Sea of Galilee. The Sea of the Dead. What causes the mighty difference between these two neighboring bodies of water? Not the River Jordan, for this river empties the same good water into both. Not the soil in which the seas lie, for it is the same. Not the country or climate round about, for both lie in Palestine.

What is the difference? Only this. The Sea of Galilee receives but does not keep the Jordan. For every drop that flows into this sea, another drop flows out—flows out to the second connecting sea. But the second sea is shrewder, hoarding its income jealously. It will not be tempted into any generous impulse. Every drop it gets, it keeps. The Sea of Galilee thus gives and lives. The second sea gives nothing. Hence, it is named the Dead. This is the story behind the two seas in Palestine.

It is also the story behind our celebration this morning. These young men are here today only because of the generosity of someone else. Someone who, like the Sea of Galilee, gives and lives. I am speaking, of course, of you parents.

Thanks to vitamins, antibiotics, and seat belts, mothers and fathers are living longer today. But paradoxically fewer and fewer are marching down the aisle to celebrate their 25th wedding anniversary. While more and more of the people are surviving, more and more of the marriages are not.

This profession ceremony is a refreshing vote of confidence in the traditional American wedding ring. For vocations can only be nurtured in homes where love and sacrifice abound. And the public commitment of these young men today can only come about because of a similar one made years ago on a wedding day. Since that day, my dear parents, you may have known sorrow. I'm sure you have known hardship. But today you know joy. Despite your misty eyes, despite your tear-stained cheeks, you are ecstatically happy, because you are generously giving your son to God.

One poet puts it this way:

> Today, upon a bus, I saw a lovely girl with golden hair.
> I envied her, she seemed so gay, and wished I were as fair.
> When suddenly she rose to leave, I saw her hobble down
> the aisle;
> She had one leg, and wore a crutch, and as she passed—a
> smile.
> O God, forgive me when I whine.
> I have two legs. The world is mine.
>
> And then I stopped to buy some sweets.
> The lad who sold them had such charm,
> I talked with him—he seemed so glad,
> If I were late, 'twould do no harm.
> And as I left he said to me: 'I thank you, sir. You've
> been so kind.
> It's nice to talk with folks like you. You see,' he said,
> 'I'm blind.'
> O God, forgive me when I whine.
> I have two eyes. The world is mine.
>
> Later, walking down the street, I saw a child with eyes
> of blue.
> He stood and watched the others play; it seemed he knew
> not what to do.
> I stopped a moment; then I said: 'Why don't you join
> the others, dear?'
> He looked ahead without a word, and then I knew—he
> could not hear.
> O God, forgive me when I whine.
> I have two ears. The world is mine.

With legs to take me where I'd go,
With eyes to see the sunset's glow,
With ears to hear what I would know,
O God, forgive me when I whine.
I'm blessed indeed. The world is mine.

Yes, my fellow religious and parents, you are blessed indeed. And the world is yours. The world of publicly presenting Christ's message about things, people, and sex. The world of giving and living, exemplified from the Sea of Galilee to the crest of Mount Tabor. The world affirmed by St. Peter with these wonderful words: "Lord, it is good for us to be here!" And I don't think proclaiming this world is dreaming the impossible dream. Do you?

SERMON AT A SIMPLE PROFESSION

"Come follow me"

During our Lord's last journey through Judea, in the final year of his earthly life, he entered a small village between Samaria and Galilee. Tradition identifies it as Janin. Here it was that Jesus cured the ten lepers and was questioned extensively by the Pharisees on the subject of divorce. And here took place the touching scene of the mothers bringing their children to Jesus for his blessing. The disciples rebuked the mothers. Jesus heard them and was indignant and said to them, "Let the little children come to me, for of such is the kingdom of God."

The Gospel goes on to narrate that as Jesus started to leave this place, a certain young man rushed up, and falling to his knees asked, "Good master, what shall I do to gain eternal life?" Jesus replied, "If you will enter into life, keep the commandments." In wonder the young man answered, "Master, all these I have kept ever since I was a child." The Gospel tells us that Jesus, looking upon him said, "One thing is lacking to you; if you will be perfect, go sell whatever you have and give to the poor, and come, follow me." St. Mark sadly relates of the young man: "His face fell at the saying, and he went away sad, for he had great possessions." Jesus looking around, said to his disciples, "With what difficulty will they who love the things of this world enter the kingdom of heaven." Yes, the call of the world and the things of this world proved too strong for the young man in our Gospel story.

"With what difficulty will they who love the things of the world enter the kingdom of heaven."

This morning Christ once again speaks, this time to the hearts of _____ young men. Once again the voice of Christ rings out, "If you will be perfect, give up all you possess and come follow me." Unlike the young man of the Gospel story, the young men before us this morning have not only heard the voice of Christ but have answered, "Speak, Lord, for your servant hears."

They have chosen the cross of Christ. By these vows of poverty, chastity, and obedience, they choose to live as Christ their Master lived, possessing nothing in their own name, living a life of celibacy and a life of obedience to God. They have answered the call of Christ, for this morning they have pledged themselves to a life of sacrifice, a life modeled on that of their divine Master, a life of striving to be other Christs. They have chosen Christ as their model and have pledged themselves by vows. They have detached themselves by their vow of poverty from the things of this world that all their efforts may go into seeking the things of God. By their vow of chastity, they deny themselves the love of wife and children that all their love may be directed entirely to Christ. By their vow of obedience they have given up their wills that they may be directed by their religious superiors to a greater service and love of almighty God.

If sacrifice is one measure of love, surely this morning we have witnessed true love.

While these young men have pledged their lives to God, another sacrifice must be noted and praised today. The sacrifice their mothers and fathers are making, for they have returned to God the most precious gift that his love bestowed on them.

Our congratulations to our newly professed brothers. Welcome to the Order. Our thanks and our gratitude to your parents whose lives and prayers have made this day possible. Certainly the Lord Jesus and his Blessed Mother will bless them for their noble sacrifice.

In the chapel of Keble College, Oxford, hangs a famous painting, *Christ, the Light of the World* by Holman Hunt. It depicts our Lord standing at a door knocking. In his hand he holds a lantern. "Behold," he is saying, "I stand at the door and knock." When Hunt had finished his painting, he invited his fellow artists to inspect it. They viewed it carefully from this angle and that. "It is a masterpiece," they said. "But," commented one of them, "you have forgotten one thing." "What is that?" asked Hunt. "You have forgotten to place a knob on the door." "No," said Hunt, "I have not forgotten it. I have omitted it purposely, for that is the door of the human heart, and it opens only from within." Christ may knock at the door of your heart, and Christ may plead, but only you can let him in. Christ stood before the door of your hearts this morning. Christ knocked, and you let him in.

The happiness that is yours this morning can and will be yours throughout life, if your hearts remain open to him.

Congratulations to you, our newly professed. May your hearts be open to him all through your lives.

SERMON AT SOLEMN PROFESSION

Probably the most popular movie of the last decade was

Star Wars. Billed as a space fantasy, its undeniable attraction was due to our fascination with planets, galaxies, robots, and computers. But *Star Wars'* popularity can also be traced to another source—its theme of good versus evil. This struggle is personified by a beautiful princess and an evil villain.

Darth Vader, the dark villain, is the last knight of a once virtuous court. There he learned the secret of power. This power is exemplified by utilizing a ray of brilliant light like a shimmering sword. This power is known as the Force, and Vader alone dominates it. Or so he thinks until he meets Alec Guinness.

Guinness too is a knight of the long-ago court. But unlike Vader, Guinness uses the Force for good, not evil. Needless to say, before the movie ends, both men meet and fight to the death. Guinness purposely loses and dies, because by his death, he can thus transmit the Force to the princess and her friends. By this means, they eventually destroy Vader. Good triumphs. Happiness is restored. As the movie ends, above the jubilation of the princess and her friends can be heard the voice of Alec Guinness, "May the Force always be with you."

"May the Force always be with you!" If there is one prayer all of us this afternoon offer for Brother _____, it is this magnificent wish from *Star Wars*. Here is a young man committing himself for life to the Force present in this solemn profession ceremony. Here is a young man publicly announcing that his love for Christ is such a Force that he will permanently live poverty, celibacy and obedience within the Catholic tradition. Here is a young man reaffirming his baptismal commitment by a unique religious commitment that is destined to remain the Force in his life forever.

Forever? This perpetuity of commitment is sharply questioned today. Isn't it rash, naive, and foolish for Brother _____ to pretend that the permanent commitment he will profess this afternoon is possible? Isn't the concept of permanence, perpetuity, and foreverness an absurdity? After all, 980,000 couples who pledged perpetuity procured divorces last year. Thirty thousand Sisters and a proportionate number of priests and Brothers left their convents and rectories within the last ten years. All these people, married and single, had promised permanency in their commitments. So, is perpetuity a legitimate aspiration or is it an absurdity? Can Brother _____ really project himself without reservation into the future? Or will he end up like Goldie Hawn, who was asked in a recent TV show to voice some marriage vows. The minister said, "Goldie, repeat after me: I take this man for better or worse, for richer and poorer, in sickness and in health, until death do us part." To which Goldie replied, "No. I take this man for better, for richer, in health—until I get bored!"

The answer to the rhetorical questions listed above, of course, is obvious. Permanency is possible. Perpetuity is real. Foreverness is a word Brother _____ can use this afternoon without the slightest bit of hesitation, because of the way he looks at his future.

Brother _____ views the years ahead as a day by day living of commitment with an emphasis on deepening, savoring, and exploring. Gabriel Marcel calls this "creative fidelity." He opposes it to constancy. The first is dynamic; the second, static. The first centers on experience *within*; the second on experience *without*. The first on internals; the second, on externals. The first on quality; the second on quantity. Only creative fidelity then makes permanent commitment possible and enables a person to take one day at a time and live it as richly as possible. Only creative fidelity allows a person to give a wholehearted embrace to the present moment.

Note that I said "whole-hearted." The word "heart" lies at the very core of today's ceremony. After all, has not the heart always been considered the seat of the emotions? Scripture speaks of people "murmuring in their hearts," of the man who "lusts in his heart," and of the "clean of heart." You are advised to love the Lord "with your whole heart." We look upon the heart as much more than a muscle for pumping blood and confirm this by so many of our expressions. We say broken-hearted, and mean that the person is completely shattered. Or say "put your heart in it," and mean "get your whole self into it." We say chicken-hearted, half-hearted, cold-hearted, hard-hearted, and we mean that the one we speak of is lacking in some human quality.

The world of dolls says something useful. As far as I know, the doll-world has been free of scandal, but a while back, something shady did occur in the manufacture of Raggedy Ann dolls.

Through the years, and despite the more sophisticated doll competition, Raggedy Ann has remained a perennial favorite. The floppy, loose-limbed rag doll with the silly grin and the colorful outfit still wins the day. Girls of all ages find her lovable and see in her qualities that are irresistible. Who knows exactly why she has this charisma?

But a minor scandal took shape; counterfeit Raggedy Ann dolls hit the market. They were fake because something essential was missing. Mass production slipped up by forgetting what appears underneath the silly clothes on the chest of every *real* Raggedy Ann doll. A *heart* is painted there, and inside it a tiny printed message reads, "I love you." You could only tell the real doll by going beneath the surface to find the heart.

Creative fidelity is like that. It is the real heart of this solemn profession ceremony. If it is missing, permanency in commitment doesn't make any sense. Only creative fidelity can give significance to the perpetual promises we will soon be hearing. Only creative fidelity can give the depth, the totality, the quality of this young man's commitment to Jesus Christ. It is a commitment strikingly similar to that of a family of three I heard about recently—a mother, a father, and a small child.

Last February, this family took a trip to visit relatives in the State of Washington. It was to be a holiday vacation. But on the first evening of the trip, the family was caught in a blinding snow storm. Driving became extremely hazardous. Finally, the automobile broke down in the snow.

When, by the next day, the family was not heard from, the relatives became worried. A search party was organized, and finally the automobile was discovered. It was half buried in the snow. The father was found standing erect in front of his wife and child. He was not wearing his coat. If he could have spoken, his would have been a very heroic story. But he could not, for the father was dead.

The mother of the family was wearing two coats, her own and her husband's. She was safe and sound except in one particular. All night long, the mother had reached out with her arms to embrace her baby. Those arms were now frozen solid and had to be amputated.

And the third member of the family, the little baby? He was as hale and hearty as if he had slept in his crib back in St. Paul.

This story beautifully suggests the solemn profession ceremony you and I are witnessing this afternoon. True, Brother _____ may sometimes believe he has committed himself to an Order whose directives are as dead and lifeless as that father. True, he may sometimes believe he has professed perpetual fidelity to a community whose concerns are as frozen and amputable as the arms of that mother. But it is equally true that, remembering the baby, his commitment will continue to make sense. Jesus is alive. He is the source of creative fidelity. He is the Force behind this young Brother who today starts out on his journey to the stars, to eternity.

Our warmest congratulations to you, Brother _____.
We are honored that you belong to our community here at

_____. Our congratulations also to your proud parents, your excited family, your happy friends. Today is the first day of your new life as a solemnly professed religious. May that life be a long and happy one. May it be filled with the permanency of creative fidelity. In short, may the Force always be with you!

SERMON FOR AN AFFILIATION CEREMONY

A Chorus Line, winner of the Tony for the Best Musical of 1975, centers on a group of dancers trying out for a Broadway show. During this musical, the life styles, the career ambitions, and the personal frustrations of these otherwise anonymous dancers are spotlighted. Instead of being a bland chorus line kicking their legs with "Rockette" precision, the performers become talented individuals possessing a unique identity.

One of the most fascinating personalities is Cassie, played by Donna McKechnie. Cassie is 32, not quite a star, clutching at what may be her last chance to "make it" in the theater. Her audition is complicated, however, because of a failed love affair with the presiding choreographer. He is both ruthless and ambitious, and Cassie finds her career in his hands.

What happens? I hope I don't spoil the story for you by telling you Cassie doesn't make the final cut. She doesn't land the job. But her grief is short-lived, because in the end, she realizes there is more than one Broadway show. Where today she failed, tomorrow she might find success.

That is a fitting introduction to this morning's celebration. For here we are—men and women, priests and lay persons, friends and benefactors—gathering together to witness a ceremony of affiliation by which we welcome _____ new members into our worldwide religious family. By this ceremony our Father General in Rome and our Father Provincial here at

_____ proudly affirm to you new affiliates that what you did you did for love. Love of the Church. Love of this religious Order.

By this ceremony, we proudly affirm that what you affiliates have done, you have done firstly for love of the Church.

Many modern authors are today stressing the idea that people are the Church; that the Church is not just the Pope and his fellow bishops, but you and I as well; that everybody belongs in Peter's fragile barque. All this is true, as far as it goes. But the trouble with this assertion is that it doesn't go far enough. The Church is not just people. It is people *and* Christ. Just as the Pope and bishops are not on one side and the rest of us on the other, so the Church is not a collection of people over here, with God and Christ up there. The Church is a gathering together of human beings around one person who is both human and divine.

This concept of Church is both our problem and our glory. It is our problem, because our part of the Church sometimes looks like a multiplication of Archie Bunkers and Mary Hartmanns rather than of Christ. It is our glory, because we are the Body of Christ, and we have the power to show the face of Christ to the world. Vatican II put it this way: "Christ is the light of the world, and his light must shine on the face of the Church. The Church is a sacrament, a living sign, of Christ."

In a real sense, you affiliates are here today because you have been such a living sign of Christ in his Church today. You are a sign that through his Church, we not only deliver Christ's message, we also shape his image. In an age trying to separate Jesus from his Church, in an age proclaiming that a Christian can *love* God but not the Church, in an age affirming that the role of the Church lies in making known to others *what* Christ says rather than show others *who* Christ is, you have been a sign, a witness to this most important unity. To love God *is* to

love his Church. God and the Church are one. Jesus left us a
seamless robe on Calvary. So it is not a case of either/or.
Rather, it is a case of both/and. What I do for love of Christ, I
also do for love of his Church.

Hans Kung points this up quite lucidly. He notes that
what divides the just inside the Church from the just outside
the Church is a "believing hope." Addressing himself to this
point in a magazine article shortly before his death, Bishop
James Pike commented that he was leaving the Episcopal
Church because "Believing hope for the Church is precisely
what I no longer possess." Note well the sequence here. First
Pike lost his believing hope in the Church. Then he departed
from the Church.

You new affiliates are being honored today, because you
have shown the world that the Church of Jesus is our believing
hope, that his Church is our light on the mountain top, our
yeast in the dough, our seed planted in the earth. Without this
visibility, there can be for us Catholics no viability.

By this ceremony, we proudly affirm that what you affiliates have done, you have done secondly for love of the
_____ Order.

Fulton Sheen once remarked that the reason St. Augustine lives on is because of his closeness to two great realities:
God and people. Augustine was close to God because he lived
in his Presence. He was close to people because he experienced
his own human defects.

This closeness to God made Augustine a man of prayer
and of extraordinary apostolic activity. As Bishop of Hippo, he
sometimes preached twice a day. In one two-hour sermon he
alluded to the insufferable heat and the discomfort of his
congregation. His sermons average anywhere from one-half
to one-and-a-half hours. He is known to have preached seven
days in succession. Many are the places in his writings where
Augustine complains of lack of time. What he says of Varro

applied to himself as well: "He read so much it was a wonder he had time to write, and wrote so much it was a wonder he had time to read." In fact, the literary activity of the last four years of Augustine's life extended to twelve works. In all, he authored ninety-three works, more than two hundred and fifty epistles, and hundreds of sermons. His literary output is six times that of Cicero's. Because he was close to God, he truly was a man of prayer and a man of amazing apostolic activity. But Augustine was also close to people.

This closeness to humans assured him of remaining an ordinary person who recognized the need for compassion, care, and love in his life. Historians tell us the Bishop of Hippo possessed a delicate constitution, was by no means robust, and was occasionally worn out and run down by the burden of his work. This man of nervous but determined disposition completely collapsed in 410, twenty years before his death, and was ordered to rest the entire summer. He found himself subject to the infirmities familiar to you and me. He was afflicted with varicose veins, plagued by pleurisy, possessed a surprisingly weak voice, was vexed by chronic hoarseness, and could be heard only with difficulty at times in the cathedral at Carthage. Being close to people, he was aware of the need of care in his life.

We try to emulate St. Augustine in his closeness to both God and people. To God by our prayer and apostolic activity. To people by being concerned about them, by caring for them, by loving them. It is for this reason that the insignia, the coat of arms, the heraldry of the Augustinian Order depicts a heart resting on a book. The book represents the Scriptures, wherein Augustine found the source of his prayer and activity. And the heart is the symbol of Augustine's humanity, which caused him to care, to love, to be concerned about people.

Today, we inscribe your names in another book, the official directory of this religious Order. Today we give you our hearts and promise a remembrance in our love and prayers forever. Your closeness to God and people are well known. We have benefited so much from your dedication, your generosity, and your encouragement. May this book and this heart inspire you even more to follow the Spirit in being close to both God and people. To God through prayer and apostolic zeal. To people by possessing a caring and loving human heart.

BACCALAUREATES AND COMMENCEMENTS

SERMON FOR GRADUATION DAY

A short passage from *The Education of Henry Adams*, who was the great-grandson of our second President, is a favorite of mine. It goes like this: "Nothing is so worthless in education as the accumulation of knowledge in the form of inert facts and the sterile compilation of things known."

It would seem, then, that a Catholic education cannot leave us inert and indifferent. It cannot leave us atrophied, much less apathetic, Catholics. Otherwise Alfred North Whitehead's remark that "knowledge keeps no better than fish" would be true of our education, our world, our life.

In our twentieth-century era of speed, power, and change, one can ask oneself, "Whatever happened to that old-time religion?" As the theme for your graduation day, we speak quite candidly about three major problems that can block your educational path to sanity and sanctity in our modern world.

First, hurry. Contemporary man, always in a hurry, indeed is a very foolish person. The English poet, William Wordsworth, said of the rush of our life style, "The world is too much with us; late and soon, getting and spending, we lay waste our powers: little we see in Nature that is ours; we have given our hearts away, a sordid boon!"

We must realize that we have been created by God in both his space and his time. We cannot turn back the hands of the clock. Neither can we turn those hands ahead. If we try to do so, we only make consummate fools of ourselves. That is why St. Paul could well tell the people of Corinth that the present, the *now*, is the acceptable time for our salvation.

But the older you get, you will be more likely to say, "We haven't got the time." We are rushing frantically about, looking for time. Did it ever occur to you that we should look inside ourselves where God is? Instead of being so much in awe of that fellow in the mirror, would it not be wiser to allow ourselves to be transformed by God's efforts? After all, day by day, we recite the prayer of all Christian peoples, the *Our Father*, and we say those powerful words, "Thy will be done on earth as it is in heaven."

The second major problem is worry. So much talk today is about the threat of pollution—air pollution, food pollution, water pollution, and noise pollution. But the real threat is psychological pollution in the form of worry. The worrier of today reminds one of the perpetually complaining hypochondriac who had carved on his tombstone the inscription, "See, I told you I was sick!"

Another intriguing story tells of an atheist who one day decided to climb a high mountain. He got up to the top all right, but slipped while climbing back down. As he plummeted downward, he desperately grabbed a thin branch protruding from the side. He hung thousands of feet up the mountain. He looked down and could see no one. He looked up and saw the same. Looking down again, he loudly cried out, "Is there anyone down there who can help me?" No answer. So our friend looked up and asked the same question, "Is there anyone up there who can help me?" At that a voice came from heaven, "I can help you." Overwhelmed, our atheist friend queried, "Who are you?" "I am God," came the response. "Will you help me?" "Yes," said the Lord, "but first I want to know if you will do whatever I ask." "I will," came the reply. "Good," said the Lord. "First, do you believe in me?" "I do," said the atheist. "Second, let go of the branch." At this my friend looked all the way down. Then he looked up again and cried out,

"Who else up there can help me?" Instead of trusting, he worried.

In today's world of fluid commitments, shifting values and sagging standards, we all can become perpetual pallbearers sizing up our newest client, if we allow ourselves. It's like the person I once met who read so much about the evils of drinking that he gave up reading. Worry kills more people than does hard work, because more people look for worry than for work. Shakespeare's Julius Caesar put it plainly when he said, "Cowards die many times before their deaths; the valiant never taste of death but once." Worry must be beaten by faith saying, "I'll do the best I can with my God-given talents and leave the rest in the hands of God." The problem is that most of us are so afraid of failing ourselves that we place too little confidence in God.

Christianity is a religion of hope. Some years ago Pope John XXIII told us not to be worriers, not to be prophets of doom, not to wring our hands despondently, not to fold them complacently, but to extend them generously to others. The more you help others, the less you will worry about yourself, for there is no beatitude for worriers except more worry.

Our third and final obstacle is scurry. By scurry I mean fickleness, indecision, dilly-dallying—the eclectic dilettantes who think that religion is a sacred smorgasbord.

The scurrier forgets the past, not realizing its tremendous importance. The philosopher of history, George Santayana, once said that "those who forget the past are condemned to repeat it." The past is important not because we live in the past, nor because we live for the past, but because we live out the past and into the present.

A recent episode in Peanuts illustrates this in a striking way. One day Lucy decides to become a psychiatrist. She turns over an orange crate and chalks up a sign, "Psychiatric Help—

Five Cents." Who stumbles along but Charlie Brown. "Lucy," he pleads, "what do you do if you don't fit in? What do you do if you don't seem to know what's going on? What do you do if you don't know what to do?" Lucy takes Charlie by the hand to the crest of a high hill which overlooks a beautiful horizon. "Do you see that world out there, Charlie Brown?", she asks. "Yes," he replies. "Is that the only world you're going to live in for the next ten or twenty years?" "Yes." "Are you sure this is the world in which you are going to live for the rest of your life?" "Yes." "There is no other—you are sure?" "Yes." "Well, in that case, won't you please live in this world, stop complaining, and give me a nickel!"

We Catholics have a heritage. It is much more than two hundred years old. It goes back much further than the Declaration of Independence. The early Christians were not bothered by a hostile environment. They had direction. They had meaning. They had a keen understanding that they were a chosen people who walked in the shadow of the Lord. So, our Christian heritage comes out of our past, into our present, and walks with us into our future.

This evening, walk with the Lord, walk out of this church, walk on to higher and better things. But wherever you walk and however far you travel and however many years you journey through life, never forget your Christian education and heritage, for you walk in the shadow of the Lord, and he is walking with you. Be with the Lord, and the Lord will be with you, as he points you today towards your tomorrow.

FOR A SPECIAL OCCASION: HUMAN HANDS

My dear friends of _____, my theme tonight is "Your Hands." Such a theme might seem odd, but next to the eyes, no other part of the human body is more expressive than the hands. They mirror the mind, reveal the heart, and reflect the soul.

Our hands can spell the difference between an outstanding American and a mediocre one, between a remarkable person and a pedestrian one, between a determined worker and an apathetic quitter. How all of you use your hands is a fascinating barometer of future success or failure, because as we gather on this night of mirth and merriment, you can fold your hands complacently, wring your hands despondently, or extend your hands generously.

First, you may choose to fold your hands complacently. But your presence here is an eloquent affirmation of Don Quixote's wisdom in dreaming the impossible dream. If you use your hands well, you are a living testimony that there need not be a clash between generations, a tuning out between the young and old, between realism and idealism, between experience and enthusiasm, between love and power, between Karl Marx and St. Mark. This, despite the critics of today who fold their hands complacently, and say that to follow a star is hopeless, and then choose to sit on their hands and cry out the words of the poet Wordsworth, "The world is too much with us . . . we have given our hearts away."

Such people who fold their hands complacently are nothing but illusioned minds with make-believe plastic patches. We are caught up in the knowledge explosion, wherein the sum of human knowledge doubles itself every five years. Obviously I cannot evaluate how much of this knowledge is worth accumulating, but if you are complacent, have no fears—just fold your hands and you will accumulate nothing.

My friends, you can wring your hands constantly in depression and desperation, and sigh despondently. Look at the world, or the country, or the county you live in. It is a place of moral flabbiness and sagging standards.

But before you wring your hands despondently, listen to

the words of Robert Louis Stevenson: "Two men look out through the same prison bars; one sees the mud, and one, the stars." True, there is mud in our modern world, there is much evil. But there is much good in our world too, much excellence.

The fact is, you and I are currently in the eye of a materialistic, spiritual, intellectual, and artistic cyclone. America has never seen such expansion. We can accelerate that expansion of our nation not by wringing our hands despondently, not by being what the late Pope John XXIII called prophets of doom, not by taking to heart the humorous advice of Bob Hope, who once said, "You young men ask what advice I shall give you about going out into this wicked world? Well, here's my advice. Don't go out." If I may be so bold as to contradict this great entertainer, let me this evening say to you, "Go out! Go out into your world, your country, your city, not folding your hands complacently, not wringing your hands despondently, but extending your hands generously."

Extend your hands as you have in the past, rededicating yourself to your cause. Extend your hands to build up and not to tear down. Extend your hands today to build a better America tomorrow.

In closing, recall the song, "Look for the Silver Lining." The song is old but the thought is contemporary. I see the silver lining in your zeal for change, change in the world, in your local community, and in yourselves. Zeal is commendable, but it must have direction and discipline. Without these, zeal will flail away in a hundred different directions and eventually die of exhaustion.

I see the silver lining in your enthusiasm for new ideas, innovations, and institutions. While enthusiasm is commendable, it must be controlled or it will run far ahead of what is possible and then quickly degenerate into cynicism, criticism, and despair.

I see the silver lining in your commitment to people. But

true commitment cannot be a free-wheeling thing. It must respond to a hierarchy of values and priorities. If it has no intellectual direction, you will wake up some day to find your broken personalities on the altar of some very strange gods.

Tonight my warmest congratulations on your successful banquet. My congratulations on your noted achievements, your devotion of time and talent, your happy faces. As you walk out of this hall tonight, determined to renew your intentions to be givers rather than takers, I ask you to do but two things: think and look. Think back upon what I said about your hands. Take a good look at your hands. Will you fold them complacently, wring them despondently, or extend them generously?

GOD AND COUNTRY

The place is Sebastea, a small, insignificant town in Armenia. The time is March of the year 320. Forty soldiers of the famous Thundering Legion of the Roman Army stand before the Emperor Licinius. Many times before, these brave soldiers have stood in the presence of the emperor. They even have received decorations for their valor. But this time something is different and there will be no decorations. This time there will be death.

These forty soldiers have just confessed their Christianity. They have appeared before the emperor to proclaim their Catholicism. And an imperial edict, issued at Milan, states that all who profess to be Catholics should be killed.

Licinius, the emperor, is angry. He is not pleased that so many of his finest soldiers should profess Christianity. After all, these men are members of his crack Thundering Legion. He must make an example of them. He must devise the cruelest sort of punishment. Suddenly an idea hits him.

The cold in Armenia is severe, especially in March when

the north wind rages. Near the walls of the city is a small lake that is frozen hard. Upon this lake, the prisoners are condemned to stand naked night and day. Either they will renounce their faith or freeze to death.

Three days and nights pass in this manner. At the end of the third day, one of the Christian soldiers gives in to the emperor. He asks to be brought to the shore. There he offers incense to the Roman gods. Then the Romans help him into a warm bath. But the reaction of the heat after the intense cold is too great. The traitorous Christian dies in the bath. He thus loses the life he has striven to save.

My young Catholics, you are today facing a challenge similar to that faced by those forty Roman soldiers over 1600 years ago. You may not belong to the Thundering Legion, but today you have been commissioned as officers in the army of Jesus Christ. You may not ever be commanded to offer incense to pagan gods, but from today onward you will be asked to profess your Catholic faith more openly. You may never have to stand on your own two feet and decide between freezing or taking a warm bath, but you do have to stand on your own two feet and meet the challenge of the largely pagan world in which you live. This challenge will mark you as either brave or cowardly, as either loyal or traitorous, as either similar to the thirty-nine who persevered, or the one who quit.

The challenge facing you today is one involving survival. It is a challenge for education, for God, and for country.

Your first challenge is for education, especially now that you are progressing toward more classroom space in your school. By that challenge to education the students here are being educated not only mentally, but morally and spiritually as well. And this education of the spirit is the fruit of Catholic grammar school education.

It has been estimated that out of every four Catholics who go to secular institutions, one falls away from the faith completely, two become mediocre Catholics, and the fourth ordinarily becomes an outstanding Catholic. The reason for success or failure involves the challenge presented.

Did you ever wonder why it is that some Catholics go astray? They stop going to Mass and the sacraments. They swear, cheat, steal. Some even are arrested and sent to prison. Why? The answer is easy: these men and women have not met the challenge of their Catholic education. They have placed knowledge of the world above love of God. They have imbibed only the mental part of their education, not the spiritual and moral.

Last year in this country, 5,262,105 pupils attended Catholic elementary schools. Can you imagine the impact on America if all would become outstanding Catholics? They should, for they face the same challenge as you, a challenge for God.

Your Catholic challenge is also a challenge for country. Do you recall from your study of history the name, Napoleon? He lived in the early 1800's and conquered vast areas for France. He united Europe for the first time since Charlemagne. But he had a strange quirk. He thought he was born under a lucky star. He felt this star was his destiny. Whatever he did, wherever he went, he believed he was following his destiny, following his star.

As Catholics, we have been, in the words of a popular song, "Born Free." We too have all been born under a special star and have a special destiny. It is the destiny of the Space Age. Today in this country you are living in a condition that we may characterize by saying, "No one ever had it so good." You live in the 20th century. You stand on the threshold of the nuclear power age and the age of interplanetary travel and communication. Unheard-of knowledge and unimagined adventures await you. You enjoy the highest standard of living that people of any time and any place ever enjoyed. And you have more creature comforts, more leisure, and more opportunity than men and women anywhere ever had. In short, you may be said to be living in the "Blast-Off" stage of a new world and a new era.

Is this not a challenge for any Catholic? No one has ever had it so good. But perhaps no one will ever have it so tough. For the competition in our nation today is keen. It is a cutthroat competition that demands truly educated men and women who realize the challenge of the times and do battle. It requires Catholics who foresee that the very roots of this new era of secularism and materialism could become a trap laid by pagan forces to imprison their resolve to follow Christ.

Here then is the challenge of your Catholic education. It is a challenge for God and for country. Allow me to conclude, if you will, by relating the story of a priest who a few years ago stood at night in an outdoor stadium in California. The stadium was illuminated by hundreds of flood lights. The priest was speaking to a group of teenagers. He was saying almost the same things I have been saying about the challenge of your Catholic education.

Then this priest did a remarkable thing. To demonstrate how each teenager present could affect the world he lived in, the priest asked that all the lights in the stadium be turned off. Then he asked each teenager to strike one match. At first there was silence. Then a chorus of scratching sounds. Then little lights began to appear all over the stadium. Before long the playing field was surrounded by a huge flame of light; it was one light coming from a large number of individual matches.

The priest proved his point. He was Father James Keller of the Christophers. And his concluding message was, "It is better to light one match than curse the darkness."

That should be the motto of all Catholics. Light the match of your challenge for God and for country. It is basically the same challenge that faced the forty soldiers of the Thundering

Legion on that icy lake in Armenia. Thirty-nine of those soldiers accepted the challenge and conquered. One rejected it and failed. What will your choice be?

THREE PATHS: LOGOS, PATHOS, ETHOS

The American philosopher Mortimer Adler considers three qualities essential to leadership in our nation. They are: Logos, the path of reason; Pathos, the path of people; Ethos, the path of faith.

With these in mind, I would like you to take a journey with me today as Americans over these three paths.

First, the path of Logos, the path of reason, Americans with reason. Over 200 years ago, George Washington and his colonial army spent a cold winter of bitterness and near-despair at Valley Forge. This was perhaps the nadir of the American revolution, the most trying of times for the poorly clothed army and the new nation it represented. But despite, or perhaps because of, the lessons learned at Valley Forge, the Americans prevailed and an experiment in democracy began, infused with the pride and optimism of our founders.

Remembering that society of so long ago, wrapped in the myths and legends of our bedtime stories and grade school civic classes, we think of a simpler world, a rural society of farmers, merchants, and craftsmen. Practicality and thrift were the essential colonial virtues.

David Reisman of Harvard, in his book *The Lonely Crowd*, says that today our affluent American society regards a person as a statistic, a number, a zip code. It is a society that has lost sight of man's dignity in this push-button world. It is a society that dehumanizes people faster than it devaluates the dollar, the very dollar bill that shows the simplicity and faith of those early years. On one side are the familiar "In God We Trust," and beneath a pyramid, the motto that tells us exactly what they thought these United States represented, "Novus Ordo Seclorum"—a new order of the ages.

Americans who do not use their logos, their reason, risk becoming simply vacuous. Today we are caught up in a knowledge explosion in which the sum of human knowledge doubles every five years. Obviously I cannot evaluate how much of this knowledge is worth accumulating, but if you are a complacent American and never use your intellect, have no fear, just fold your hands, and you will accumulate nothing. For you there will not be any "new order of the ages." Always remember, ancient Rome gained the world and lost her soul. Now modern America clings to her manifest destiny, while the destiny of her soul is hardly manifest.

Second, the path of Pathos, the path of people. From six million people, we Americans have swelled to more than 230 million. From a nearly homogenous group of Anglo-Saxons, we have split into many diverse and often disagreeing groups. From a former "colony" we have become an awesome military establishment and world power. From a society that emphasized thrift, we have become a nation of conspicuous consumers.

But this materialistic progress is one of the causes of our dilemma. Affluence and sophistication are the order of things today. We are intoxicated by our achievements. To the world have we perhaps become characterized by hate and greed? Are we a nation that has forgotten how to love? Someone has said that America will perish not from the bomb, but from boredom. History reminds us that the love of power forever threatens the power to love. Despite the plethora of verbiage about togetherness, ingrouping, and sense of community; despite the strident cries of our hippies, flower children and love-ins; despite the oceans of ink poured out about personalism; you and I are living in a cold, loveless age.

Today change, constant, ubiquitous, and ever accelerating, has become the most striking feature of our society. Alvin Toffler's *Future Shock* stresses the rapidity of change in today's world, alterations in society, thinking, life style, education, family, and churches.

In our world today we have seen perhaps more clearly than any other age, the death of permanence. Many people today accept news and change with relative ease. It is an amusing but frightening fact that the speed of life, the throw-away attitude, and the temporary relationships of today, almost make suspect any Gibralter-like attitudes or clinging to tradition.

In our age of *angst*, rapid change brings even more worry—the fear of a second great depression, the possibility of further involvement in another "small" war, the up-close terror of crime in our cities. So many things contribute to our gnawing sense of anxiety.

In these past years, you have grown and learned, hoped and aged with all of America. We have been confronted with our own limits, the limits of our power in Vietnam, the limits of our resources in the energy crisis, the limits of our leaders in the Watergate scandal. We have seen that in some cases our vast natural wealth has fed the very passions our founders had identified with a decadent European aristocracy—greed, arrogance, and the enjoyment of wasteful luxury in the presence of acute deprivation.

My dear friends, the path of the Pathos tells us of sensitivity and feeling, that we are indeed people who need people. The Congo, Cuba, Chile, Cyprus, El Salvador, and China really do matter intensely. The stock market jumps with every rumble anywhere and this tells us that today, economically and politically, the world is a global village.

We must be aware of the difficulties, differences, and needs of others, beginning with the family and our neighbors. Ought not Philadelphia, Mississippi be a concern of ours as well as Philadelphia, Pennsylvania? Ought not we, like Christ, have compassion upon the multitude, upon the people who, like us, really need people? As Americans, we have so much to give, for indeed we are the luckiest people in the entire world. Third, the path of Ethos, the character of the country. Only too well has modern America learned that brains are not enough to run a society. Religious strength must be paramount. We Americans are often impoverished by possessions and governed by machines. We have cleared the forests and even split the atom, but the more we outwardly master nature and the universe, the more God overwhelms our hearts.

The Logos, the Pathos, and the Ethos are the tools with which we must work to achieve new goals that are really the old American goals of self-reliance and economic self-denial, even austerity. But the most important is the Ethos, the moral fiber of our nation.

Reaching across the two centuries that yawn between us and Washington and Jefferson, we can link minds and hearts with those men and relearn from them the basic colonial or pioneer virtues: a vision leading to faith, a resignation leading to hope, a compassion leading to charity, patience to realize that quick and facile solutions are an illusion, thrift to use all our resources wisely and well, courage to be determined to resist evil in ourselves and in our government.

In the Federalist Papers, James Madison makes this point: "There is a degree of depravity in mankind which requires a certain degree of distrust; but there are other qualities which justify a certain portion of esteem and confidence. Republican government presupposes the existence of these qualities in a higher degree than any other form."

What Madison tells us today is that we simply cannot do without these virtues as we near the year 2000. The time has indeed come for a return to a simpler, less wasteful style of life.

We, who have been in many ways a generation of affluence, must learn to do with less, for we have been given much, and much more will be asked of us.

Let the modern person see what we are searching for, and then the sad cry of Gandhi will not be needed, "If only you Christians were more like Christ."

Modern Christianity will not be building a new city. Instead it will be holding together the old, continuing, renewing, and rebuilding the city of man and leading it back to the city of God. There can be no "Novus Ordo," but one can rekindle the fires of sacrifice and hope that helped light the shining "new order of the ages" two centuries ago. It will demand imagination, wisdom, restraint, and plain hard work, but it can be accomplished through Logos, your reason; Pathos, your sensitivity; and most of all, Ethos, your character.

We must adapt in order to survive. Like Washington and Jefferson of old, we must sacrifice in order to win. As we draw near to the year 2000, let us not be embarrassed to admit that we Americans can be a very good people. Nonetheless, it's going to be a long, hard pull. Let us begin. In the words of President John Fitzgerald Kennedy's inaugural address, "Here on earth God's work must truly be our own."

EUCHARIST AND TODAY'S CATHOLIC

On September 8, 1971, in the John F. Kennedy Center for Performing Arts in Washington, D.C., a select audience attended a premiere of Leonard Bernstein's "Mass." Since that date, Bernstein's "Mass" has been seen by thousands of enthusiastic spectators.

Did I say "enthusiastic"? "Puzzled" might be a more accurate adjective, for Bernstein's "Mass" seems to be a constant contradiction. First come parts of the Latin Mass: *Gloria, Confiteor, Credo.* Then come three English songs that tell us why the

Latin parts are obsolete. At the beginning, a denim-clad young man begins to put on his vestments, piece by piece. But he must repeat the "Let us pray" louder each time because the people around the altar seem interested in talking only to each other. When he sings the Confiteor, they respond with the song, "Why I cannot confess." When he sings the Creed, they counter with, "I'll believe in God if God will believe in me!"

Gradually the dichotomy between priest and people becomes more and more evident. They are not here to celebrate Mass. By the time the Offertory comes, there is a mad scramble below the priest on the floor.

Finally the priest climbs to the top of the altar and rends his garments. No one pays him any attention. Then he takes the bread and wine and hurls them down onto the floor. There can be no celebration, he sings, because there is no community.

Bernstein is echoing the concern of many other Americans about community in our land. Consider the words of three especially memorable citizens. "Ask what you can do for your community," urged a young President from Massachusetts. "I have a dream about community," said a crusading black minister. "I ask: Why not a community?", declared a hopeful New York Senator.

Yet the more we talk about community, the more we seem to find it lacking. In the *New York Times* the other day, I read these headlines: "Syria invades Lebanon—250 more die in Beirut." "Sixteen-year Old Visitor Mugged and Murdered in Manhattan's Central Park." "For the 5th Day in a Row, Blacks and Whites Riot in Boston's Busing Controversy." "West Point Cheating Scandal Now Involves More Than 200 Cadets."

These headlines are from one issue of one newspaper on one day. Is it any wonder the priest in Bernstein's "Mass" cries out: "There can be no celebration today, because there is no community."

Or is there? Jesus entered our world precisely to show us

that community is possible. It comes about when people work for justice and when people live with love. You and I are Jesus' followers. On this Graduation Day, are we helping to bring about this community? Are we working for justice and striving for love?

We begin to create a Christian community by working for justice. Recently a writer took the whole world and miniaturized it into a town of 1,000 people. Studying this world-town gives us some startling facts and figures.

In this town of 1,000, 60 people would be Americans and 940 would be of other nationalities. This is the proportion of the U.S. to the population of the world: 60 to 940.

The 60 Americans would have half the income of the entire town, with the other 940 dividing the other half. The 60 Americans would have an average life expectancy of 70 years; the other 940, less than 40 years. The 60 Americans would average 15 times as many possessions per person as all the rest of the people. They would produce 16% of the town's total food supply but consume 40%. They would spend $850 a year per family on guns, but less than $4 on religion. They would spend more money annually on the average American dog than Latin Americans, Asians, or Africans would spend on the average child.

Such inequality shows the need for justice in our world. As long as there is such a large imbalance, as long as one side can be called the "haves" and the other the "have nots," there can be no widespread Christian community. Pope Paul put it this way: "We are responsible for the poor of the world." On this, your Graduation Day, do you accept this responsibility? Will you, like Jesus, seek to create community by working for justice?

The most important way we create a Christian community is by striving for love. During the Vietnam War, Bob Hope spent much of his time in Saigon visiting the homes for children supported by charity. He handed out hundreds and hundreds of chocolate bars to orphaned youngsters.

At one large orphanage, in the center of the city, Hope had a startling experience. Most of the children eagerly grabbed his chocolate bars. Yet he noticed, out of the corner of his eye, a little girl sitting all by herself in the corner. She had a wan face and blonde curls. She had not touched her candy.

As soon as he could break away from the throng of admirers, Bob walked over to the little girl and knelt down beside her. "Now, just what can I do for you, young lady?" he asked.

Bob tells us he then heard the two saddest words he had ever heard in all his life. The little girl looked up at him and said, "Love me."

"Love me!" Is there any better way to build a community than through loving people? Henri Nouwen has said we should distinguish between curing and caring. In a community like ours, we have put so much emphasis on cure rather than care. We want to be professionals: heal the sick, help the poor, teach the ignorant, organize the scattered. But a serious temptation arises here. It is the temptation to use our expertise in a non-caring way, to become concerned with results, achievements, and outcomes, to forget that unless cure grows out of care, it can become more harmful than helpful.

Nouwen strikes a responsive chord here. The word "care" finds its roots in the Gothic "kara," which means "lament." The basic meaning of care, therefore, is to grieve, to experience sorrow, to cry out. And when we honestly ask ourselves which persons in our lives mean the most to us, how do we answer? Those who gave us advice, solutions, and cures, or those who shared our pain, touched our wounds, cried out with us when we were in pain? Obviously we answer the second. Why? Because they cared. They were silent with us in a moment of despair or confusion. They stayed with us in an hour of grief and bereavement. They tolerated not knowing, not curing, not healing, and simply were present to us.

This is what Nouwen is saying. Cure without care makes us into technicians, rulers, controllers, and manipulators. Cure without care makes us preoccupied with quick solutions, simplistic answers, sudden miracles. Cure without care makes it impossible for us to respond to our brother's and sister's psychological needs for affection, security, achievement, independence, and self-worth.

The result is alienation between two persons. Only care can bring about reconciliation of one person with another.

Surely one of the most serious illnesses of today's world is that there is too much cure and not enough care. As followers of Jesus, we can reverse that trend. We can love.

Here then are the two ways we can create Christian community. Justice will lead us to be concerned about imbalance. Love will lead us to care as well as cure.

A story I heard recently sums this up quite well. It is about a family of three who took an automobile trip last Christmas.

The father, mother, and small baby left their home in St. Paul, Minnesota and set out to visit relatives in the State of Washington. It was to be a holiday vacation. But on the first evening of the trip, the family was caught in a blinding snow storm. Driving became extremely hazardous. Finally, the automobile broke down in the snow.

When the family was not heard from the next day, relatives became worried. A search party was organized and finally the automobile was discovered half buried in the snow. The father was found standing erect in front of his wife and child. He was not wearing his coat. If he could have spoken, his would have been a heroic story. But he could not, for he was dead.

The mother of the family was wearing two coats, her own

and her husband's. She was safe and sound except in one particular. All night long, the mother had reached out with her arms to embrace her baby. Those arms were now frozen solid and had to be amputated.

And the little baby? He was as hale and hearty as if he had slept in his crib that terrible night.

I tell this story because it has a powerful message for you on this Graduation Day. Granted you are graduating into a world beset by revolution, conflict, and alienation. Granted some people are saying that justice in our community is as dead as that father. Granted critics are telling us that cure is the answer to the world's need for love, for care is as frozen as the arms of the mother. But what they don't tell us is that the baby lived. Jesus is alive. He is alive in you and me. So there can be justice and love in our community, if only we try hard enough.

Think back to that priest in Bernstein's "Mass." "There can be no celebration," he says, "because there is no community." Today you Graduates can contradict him, for this Graduation celebrates a Christian community concerned with justice and love.

A GERMAN LEGEND

A legend of old Germany tells about an old man named Bertram. He had been a monk for many years and had spent most of his time in the monastery workshop as a skilled woodcarver. All the statues in the monastery had been carved by him. The abbot one day sent for Bertram and said, "His Eminence, the Cardinal, is going to visit us soon. Everything about the monastery is prepared for him except that we still need a statue of Christ near the main altar. Can you make one for us in time?" Poor Bertram went back to his workshop and began to worry. He said to himself, "Cedarwood from Lebanon is just the thing, but I have none. There isn't a single piece of fine and costly wood in the workshop. All I have is that old piece of oak in the corner, dusty and twisted. What good is that? I wish I had a piece of cedarwood. What a fine statue I could make then." "Statue—main altar—Cardinal—piece of oak." Mumbling these words, Bertram fell asleep. The legend goes on to say that while he slept a wonderful thing happened. An angel came from heaven, picked up Bertram's tools and began to carve the old oak log in the corner. Blow by blow, the image of Christ began to be formed from the castaway piece of wood. Soon the statue was finished. The angel tickled Bertram's nose with a shaving to wake him and then vanished. Bertram was surprised. There was the statue of Christ, as large as life, standing just as if he were preaching the Sermon on the Mount. A wonderful statue and all carved out of that old piece of oak that Bertram thought was not good enough. Bertram brought the abbot and told him the story. The abbot then said quite simply to the monk, "Christ wants us to make the most of what we are, and not to dream of what we would do if things were different."

How often do you dream of great deeds that you could do if things were only different? For example, how often do you say, "If I had only lived in the time of Christ, how I would have loved him," or "When I go to high school, then I'll start being good"? If you say things like that to yourselves and neglect to change *now*, to be good *now*, you are making the same mistake that Bertram made when he wanted a cedar log from far-off Lebanon instead of the oak log in the corner. You must make the most of what you are. You must become the beautiful person God created you to be. God had a reason for making you at this time, in this place, in the home and school where you are. You must make the most of it and not dream of how good you could be if things were different.

A human person is the only being in this world who asks questions, and the most important questions he or she asks are those put to oneself. Each one puts the questions to himself or herself somewhat differently, but all of us are in some way asking, "How am I to live? How am I to understand and evaluate my life?" Time and again we desert or fall short of our own goals. We act against our own best interests. We are at war within ourselves. We are constantly being threatened with not finding our answer, with not recognizing it if we do find it, or failing it if we do recognize and pursue it. What is the answer? Who is the answer? Christ is. For two thousand years humankind, in numberless millions, has found in Jesus of Nazareth its answers. The Christian religion proclaims that Jesus is the source of our answers and the way to them. He tells us, "I am the way, and the truth, and the life."

When we look carefully at the Gospel story, what do we find? Jesus is not what we may think he is or want him to be; he is what he and his disciples said he is. He is not just the greatest, the best, the most important person ever to come along. He is the person on whom everything and everyone else depends. The important thing about Jesus, as the New Testament gives him to us, is that he manifests to us the meaning of human life. And he illuminates life not from outside, but from inside, by living it. Christ was touched by life and affected by it. He was a real, living, breathing man. He had a human body and soul, human feelings, human problems, doubts, fears, and struggles. He ate and drank, slept and rose, was tired and troubled, smiled and wept. And we will not understand ourselves if we do not understand him.

Our challenge this evening and for life is to live Christ. Our world is in darkness. People live in fear. They live with so many lies they cannot recognize the truth. There are few sound values in our society. Many do not take religion seriously. There is little respect for one another.

You graduates are challenged to take a light into this darkness, the light which is Christ himself. I hope you graduates will open yourselves to the Spirit of Christ. Without it there is little you can do; with it there is little you cannot do.

You are on the threshold of a new beginning in your life. Like Christ, you have to convince others mostly by showing them that you mean what you say. You must be ready to stake everything on the truth of the Gospel. It is living Christ so completely and with such conviction that the world around you is influenced and, I hope, persuaded that what you say and do is the truth. Whether you actually do influence and persuade others is not ultimately in your power. You can only try.

Tonight, Christ asks you a question: "Are you with me?" Everyone likes to be different and special; no one likes to be just ordinary. And indeed each one of us is unique and special. No two leaves, no two drops of water are alike, just as no two people are alike. This means your answer to God's question must be personal. Your whole education is there to help you, plus your talents, gifts, and personality. Your parents and teachers have chipped away at your failures and mistakes so that the image of Christ in you comes through. "Christ wants us to make the most of what we are, and not to dream of what we would do if things were different."

As Phillips Brooks says, "Be such a man, and live such a life, that if every man were such as you, and every life a life like yours, this earth would be God's paradise."

Congratulations! May you go with Christ and be with Christ forever in your life's journey!

LIFE, LOVE, LAW

The modern person is a paradox, a problem, and an enigma. On the one hand contemporary Americans give much attention to improving the quality of life. We seek to ameliorate our health care service, to eliminate poverty, and to increase our educational efforts. Ecology drives, anti-war movements, and efforts to abolish capital punishment are commonplace. On the other hand, never has the threat to life been greater. Abortion on demand is the law of the land, and euthanasia and sterilization are frequently in the news. People are more and more ambivalent and confused.

This real-life paradox is tragic, as tragic as what I see happening to the three mainstays of contemporary American existence—life, love and law.

First, life. Recently I had the good fortune to see a movie entitled "Giving Birth," a twenty-minute Defense Department documentary about what one should do if a woman comes to her time and there is no doctor in the house.

I don't know how many of you have witnessed a live birth, but what I find tragic today is the number who are not interested and who hold a philosophy of life that is a throwback to Germany of the Thirties. These persons espouse the utilitarian ethic that declares, "What is useful is good."

This ethic has made fetal life cheap today. It has brought on The Silent Holocaust. An estimated 1,340,000 legal and illegal abortions were performed in the United States last year. This means that in one operating room surgeons are laboring to save a twenty-one week old baby, and in the next other surgeons are killing another twenty-one week old fetus.

This means a Caesarean section that, as an operation, can

save mother and child, can also, as an abortion, kill the child.

This means life, movement, pulse at nineteen weeks and a plastic-bagged garbage can full of dead babies at twenty-two weeks.

"What is useful is good." The euphemisms drip like sweet cyanide. The good death . . . the peaceful death . . . death with dignity . . . the legal death.

Could the "what-is-useful-is-good" mentality lead to such horror in the United States? Not so long as we are allowed to speak out (the priests in Germany could not). Not so long as right-to-life Americans can dispute and protest (the citizens in Germany could not). Not so long as we can look with sadness on the tragedy that happened to a young college woman about whom I recently read.

It happened this spring at one of our midwestern universities. The senior college woman left the campus for a stroll in the surrounding woods on a lovely spring day. The blue sky and cordial sun, the bright buds on the trees, and the cheerful chirping of the birds, all conspired to make one happy, vigorous, and thrilled to be alive.

Near sundown, a farmer passing by the woods thought he saw something strange dangling from one of the trees. He stopped his team of horses and investigated. The young woman's body was hanging from a stout lower limb. With the belt from her coat she had made a clumsy noose and hanged herself. At her feet lay an open book, face upwards. On the flyleaf the girl had written these lines: "Life is a joke, and all things show it. I thought so once, but now I know it."

This incident is unspeakably sad because this girl didn't know the value, sanctity and dignity of human life. She didn't know the intense relationship existing between life and love.

This brings me to my second point, love, and here I must refer to the February pastoral letter, in which the bishops of the United States made a startling statement: "One of the dangers of a technological society is a tendency to adopt a limited view of man, to see man only for what he does. Such a tendency overlooks the source of man's dignity . . . the powerful fact that he is made in the image of God."

This is what we are facing in the United States today.

The utilitarian ethic of "what is useful is good."

The belief that man holds his dignity only in functioning for other persons.

The denial of worth and dignity that comes from being a child of a loving God.

I heard a story the other day about just such a child. His name was Joseph, and he was retarded. The older of two children, the difference between Joseph and his active, bubbling, effervescent younger brother was most apparent. His father particularly noticed this difference and often argued about what had he done to deserve the slow, retarded child. Many times Joseph and his brother heard his father shout out loud about the boy's lack of value, his low place in the family, his meaningless role in society.

One evening his father was finishing such a tirade with the question, "What can he do? What can he be in life?" Just then, the door burst open and Joseph came in, scratched, bruised, and bleeding, followed by his little brother. "What happened?" the mother demanded. The younger brother responded, "Some big boys were throwing rocks at me down the street. Joseph saw them and ran over to me. Then he stood in front of me, protecting me from the stones. I'm so lucky to have such a loving brother." At this, the mother turned to the father. "Now you see," she said, "now you know what Joseph can do. He can be! He can love!"

Love gives that indefinable quality to life. Love enables a person to live fully.

Any wonder our bishops railed against "a limited view of man"?

Any wonder they replied so vehemently to the Supreme Court decision that took love out of life by permitting abortion on demand?

This brings me to my third point, law. Certainly our bishops' reply to the striking down of the anti-abortion law is startling. You are familiar with the text. Are you as familiar with the tone? "We reject the decision. It lacks judicial force. The Supreme Court is wrong and accordingly *we shall not serve*" (emphasis added).

For years the average American Catholic simply did not believe that his government would ever do anything opposed to the common good, to the perennial dictates of the natural law. We bedecked our churches with Old Glory and thus symbolized our conviction that in the U.S.A., God and country would always stand together. Faith and patriotic obedience were at least complementary virtues. Our government was the servant of God, and that's all there was to it.

Today we know that's not all!

Today we know that the American government is able to oppose itself to the natural law and the authentic common good.

Today we know why the bishops could declare: "Whenever a conflict arises between the law of God and any human law, we are held to follow God's law."

For two hundred years the American Catholic believed in his government and thought that the political order could be trusted. That's why the comfortable meld of "Catholic" and "American" has been disastrously upset.

What about us? Each one of us here should be advocates of life, love, and law. Is the utilitarian ethic of life a subtle part of our belief? Is the concept of loving a person because of what he does perhaps infringing on our dignity as children of God?

Is the shock of an American law utterly opposing the common good galvanizing us into action?

Think of the tragic ambiguity of America's life, love and law. Take as your own, the words of the unknown poet who wrote:

Today, upon a bus, I saw a lovely girl with golden hair.
I envied her, she seemed so gay, and wished I were as fair.
When suddenly she rose to leave, I saw her hobble down
    the aisle.
She had one leg, and wore a crutch, and as she passed—a
    smile.
O God, forgive me when I whine.
I have two legs. The world is mine.

And then I stopped to buy some sweets.
The lad who sold them had such charm,
I talked with him—he seemed so glad,
If I were late, 'twould do no harm.
And as I left he said to me: 'I thank you, sir. You've
    been so kind.
It's nice to talk with folks like you. You see,' he said,
    'I'm blind.'
O God, forgive me when I whine.
I have two eyes. The world is mine.

Later, walking down the street, I saw a child with eyes
    of blue.
He stood and watched the others play; it seemed he knew
    not what to do.
I stopped a moment; then I said, 'Why don't you join
    the others, dear?'
He looked ahead without a word, and then I knew—he
    could not hear.
O God, forgive me when I whine.
I have two ears. The world is mine.

With legs to take me where I'd go,
With eyes to see the sunset's glow,

With ears to hear what I would know,
O God, forgive me when I whine.
I'm blessed indeed. The world is mine.

Yes, my friends, you and I are fortunate indeed, for the
world is ours, the world of life, love, and law.

RECONCILERS OF THE WORLD—
AN IMPOSSIBLE DREAM?

(AN ADDRESS TO THE KNIGHTS OF COLUMBUS)

This afternoon, my dear Knights, it might be well to impress the magnificent theme song of another knight, Don Quixote, deep within our hearts. It is "The Impossible Dream." After all, here we are—men and women, priests and laity, officers and members—gathered together at our annual Knights of Columbus convention. According to Webster, a convention is "a coming together, an act of convening; a uniting for the purpose of reconciliation." But critics hasten to assure us that what we are doing here is, in reality, a charade, that in convening this assembly of Knights from around the world, we really are dreaming an impossible dream, that to talk today of unity, togetherness, and reconciliation is following a star that is both hopeless and far!

"Consider the last ten years," our critics urge. "If anything, this past decade has been characterized by division, not reconciliation; by alienation, not unity."

But you and I come together as a sign of unity, togetherness, and reconciliation! A lot of people this afternoon live in cities where it is not safe to walk the streets at night. Many live in countries in which the number of births is rapidly being equaled by the number of abortions. Many live in a world of demilitarized zones—not just North and South Vietnam, but black, white, and red America, India and Pakistan, East and West Berlin, and Northern and Southern Ireland!

So what's the sense of holding this convention? Is not such a meeting really dreaming an impossible dream? How can such a display of unity really speak to an age that prefers riots to reason, pot to patriotism, and hate to love?

How? Perhaps in this way. The more divided, confused, and alienated our world, the more meaningful is the affirmation of unity expressed by our convention today. The more we hear about revolution, the more necessary becomes reconciliation. The more people fret about what's wrong with America, the more necessary it becomes for us to tell the world what's right with America.

I grant you that as Knights of Columbus we are experiencing diversity. A few years ago, for example, we thought that if one devotion in the Church would always remain inviolate, that devotion was the rosary. Today, with some confused priests telling us to throw away our rosaries because it is really a prayer for illiterates, we don't speak that way anymore. A few years ago we used to say that if one class of people in the Church was totally dedicated, that class was our priests and sisters. But today, with priests and sisters leaving in such unprecedented numbers, we don't speak that way anymore.

A few years ago we used to say that Catholic education was unparalleled and certainly going to survive forever. A Catholic school for every parish was the goal. Today, with arguments raging about the relevancy of these schools and with so many closing, we don't talk that way anymore. Finally, a few years ago we used to say that if there were one sign of a good Catholic, it was unswerving fidelity to the Church. But today with distinctions being made between the institutional church and the underground church, between the hierarchical church and the charismatic church, people are asking, "Has anyone seen the real Church lately?"—and so we don't speak that way anymore.

So where does all this leave us? It leaves us with a gap. But my point is this. What about showing people the bridge for that gap? What about talking of unity in an age of disunity? What about being signs of hope and reconciliation? What about building a bridge? It must be a bridge dynamically focusing on the person of Jesus Christ.

Jesus is alive. He is in our presence today as a sign of hope, unity, and reconciliation. So rather than despair about all the divisions, why not concentrate our efforts on proclaiming Jesus, the sign of reconciliation, to our world?

There is no denying the fact that Jesus is exploding into our contemporary scene in an apocalypse of sight and sound undreamed of five years ago. Wide-eyed young girls and earnest young men badger businessmen and shoppers on Hollywood Boulevard, near the Lincoln Memorial, and along Fifth Avenue with breathless exhortations for witnessing to Christ. Christian coffeehouses are opening across the country with such revealing names as "The Way Word" in Greenwich Village, "The Catacombs" in Seattle, "The I Am" in Spokane. Communal Christian hostels are multiplying like loaves and fishes. Bibles abound. Telephones are answered with "Jesus Loves You" instead of "Hello." In fact, Jesus plays are on Broadway; Jesus songs are on popular radio stations; Jesus sweatshirts and buttons are sold. These things are inundating our country, our culture, and our consciousness.

Last Christmas, you could give someone you love a gift that could put him "with Jesus every minute of the day." It was a Jesus watch and it sold for $19.95. In the words of the advertiser, "Our Jesus watch comes with the Savior's likeness, in the race of your choice, complete with a revolving crimson heart." The businessman responsible for the Jesus watch, it is reported, got his inspiration from a rubber, squeaking Buddha doll.

Outrageous? Not if you make your living on Madison Avenue. Jesus has become such a folk hero and such a social phenomenon in the 70's that American merchandising has accorded him a place in our pop culture alongside Mickey

Mouse and Spiro Agnew. Paradoxically you may remember
that five years ago John Lennon of the Beatles rock group
tossed off a remark that his singing group was more popular
than Jesus. Critics blasted him for glib irreverence, and yet he
was probably speaking the truth. But look at what has happened today. The Beatles no longer exist, and Jesus Christ has
become a superstar!

Obviously this is not the Jesus I am holding up to you
Knights to proclaim. Jesus Superstar is a phony and a fad. He
is here today and gone tomorrow. No, the Jesus I am propos-
ing as a symbol of reconciliation is Jesus Savior. The real Jesus.
The One who loves, inspires, cares, and heals.

Have you ever noticed how often the Gospel depicts Jesus
as a healer? His first miraculous action described by Mark is the
casting out of a devil from a man possessed. To read the New
Testament further is to follow a trail of discarded bandages,
crutches, and stretchers. Jesus' whole public life is a story of
healing—from Peter's mother-in-law's fever to Lazarus' unravelling shroud; from the woman with the hemorrhage to the
daughter of Jairus. One of the most beautiful passages is in the
fourth chapter of St. Luke. Jesus had had a busy day. He began
by teaching in the synagogue, and there he expelled an un-
clean spirit from a man. He then healed Peter's mother-in-law.
But he still couldn't rest. "At sunset, all who had people sick
with a variety of diseases took them to him, and he laid hands
on each of them and cured them."

This is the Jesus we Knights of Columbus should
proclaim, the healing Jesus who challenges us to be reconcilers
of the world. He is the Jesus who is for all of us a Savior, not a
Superstar. He is the Jesus who validates Don Quixote's wisdom
in dreaming the impossible dream.

To heal means to make whole, to restore to health that
which was diseased, to remove the forces of evil destroying
unity among people. To heal means to bind wounds of divi-

sion, alienation, and separation. To heal means to bring peace where there is disorder, quiet where there is discord, joy where there is misery.

So many confused individuals cannot face today's world. Alienated people. Divided people. People in need of healing and reconciliation. Are we reaching out to them? Are we failing them?

Some contemporary existentialists think we are. Listen to Albert Camus: "Life is a pest-ridden existence." And Jean Paul Sartre said, "Hell does not consist in torture. Hell consists in an empty heart!"

I think, my brother Knights, these words aptly characterize the world in which we live, the gap we are being asked to bridge, and the division we are urged to heal. It is a world of an empty heart, a world that has forgotten the love only Jesus Savior can bring. Despite the plethora of verbiage about togetherness, ingroupness, and sense of belonging, despite the strident cries of our hippies and flower children, despite the oceans of ink poured forth about personalism, existentialism, and individualism, you and I are living in a loveless age. How else explain that the modern person is paralyzed with fear, filled with doubt, and alienated from other people? How else explain why the modern person has run to sex and drugs, and made our suicide rate the third highest on the face of the earth?

The grand malaise of today's age is depersonalization. Accent is on products, goods, gadgets, things, not on people. The "I—Thou" relationship of Martin Buber has become the "I—it" relationship. The Dutch theologian, E. Schillebeeckx, in fact, describes today's environment as "the age of the Exuberantly Growing It!" Erich Fromm blames America's violence on its dehumanization and loss of respect for the individual. And David Reisman, sociology professor at Harvard, talks about *The Lonely Crowd* in a recent book. You and I, he says, are part of a nameless, faceless, fragmentized, computerized society that regards man as a statistic, a zip code, and a credit card number. This society dehumanizes people even faster than it devalues the dollar bill. This society has lost sight of the individual in our push-button world of thought control, remote control, birth control, and no control. Any wonder Don Quixote's theme song begins, "To dream the impossible dream"!

As Knights of Columbus, as modern bridge-builders, as men of reconciliation, you and I must show the world that love, healing, and unity are not an impossible dream. Shortly before his tragic death, Martin Luther King made this dramatic statement: "The question we must ask ourselves today is not whether we will be extremists. Rather, the question we must ask ourselves is what kind of extremists will we be? Will we be extremists for hate or extremists for love?"

Our answer must be: extremists for love! Here is how we can portray the real Jesus to our world, the Jesus who loves, heals, and reconciles. Remember, wherever lies and half-truths are preached, there too is air pollution. Wherever suspicion and distrust are spread, there too is germ warfare. Wherever the young are taught to hate, there too is defoliation. So you and I, my brother Knights, must be extremists for love. We must be aware of our role as reconcilers of the world. We must reach out with the healing Jesus so that the tragedy of hatred in our world may gradually diminish and be replaced by worldwide peace and love.

Today there are so many people who feel alienated, unloved, and dehumanized. Will we show them the healing love of the real Jesus? Will we truly be reconcilers of the world? Will we really take to heart these concluding words of the late Richard Cardinal Cushing?

"If all the sleeping Knights will wake up;
And all the lukewarm Knights will fire up;

And all the dishonest Knights will confess up;
And all the disgruntled Knights will sweeten up;
And all the discouraged Knights will cheer up;
And all the depressed Knights will look up;
And all the estranged Knights will make up;
And all the gossiping Knights will shut up;
And all the apathetic Knights will shake up;
And all the real Knights will pray up;
Then, we will have history's greatest
        Fraternal Organization!"

The Cardinal is right. We Knights of Columbus can be reconcilers of the world. And I don't think this is dreaming the impossible dream.

Do you?

ADDRESS TO THE FRIENDLY SONS OF ST. PATRICK

You have heard, no doubt, that there are two classes of people in the world: those who are Irish, and those who wish they were Irish! With a name like McNulty, I naturally fall into the first class. So you can imagine my rapture at being privileged to spend a month on the Emerald Isle a few years ago while on vacation from my theological studies in Rome.

No banshee leaped from behind a tree to surprise me, but I did meet two fishermen, the brothers Fitzgerald, who swore that they had seen a mermaid off the coast of Kerry. No leprechaun popped up with a pot of gold, but a photographer did take my picture kissing the treasured Blarney Stone. The sun didn't shine in the sky every day of my visit, but what touch of warmth could equal the reaction of my jarvey at Killarney to what I considered a good tip: the jarvey took off his coat, threw it over the horse's head, and said to me, "Father, I'd be ashamed to let the horse see you giving me this!"

Yet, with all these memories, nothing in Ireland fascinated me more than that country's ancient Celtic monasteries. There must be hundreds of them—on islands in the Atlantic, on islands in the rivers, and alongside mountain lakes. Of some, not a single stone today remains above ground. Of others, nothing can be seen but an early gravestone or a battered cross. Several have the ruins of some old church or school. And many possess as their sole remnant, a tall, tapering building called the Round Tower.

These Round Towers are found in no other place in the world. Often stretching 250 feet in height, the solid stone structure reminds one of a huge belfrey. But the Towers could not have been used as such. They are more like impregnable castles. The doorway stands fifteen to twenty feet above the ground, the sole opening in the Tower and accessible only by a ladder.

Historians trace the function of these Round Towers back to the time of the Viking invasions. Located, as they were, near the water highways, the Irish monasteries were an easy prey to the adventurous Danes. Prosperous abbeys, like Clonmachnois, Glendalough, and Mellifont were ravaged time and time again. The monks' only defense was in flight. It does not take much imagination to picture the barbarian hordes landing on the monastery shore. The monks climb frantically through the door of their Round Tower, and the ladder is taken up, just as the first Viking, with flaming torch, appears at the barred monastic gate. What relief for the monks to find themselves secure in their fortress! What happiness at having escaped almost sure death! What peace at being able to enjoy the maximum benefit of their impregnable Tower!

In our own era you and I are experiencing much the same emotions that characterized those Irish monks in their Round Towers centuries ago. Here we are, celebrating a day on which millions of people jam the streets to wave flags honoring a saint who died over 1,500 years ago. We celebrate at a time in history so bewildering and confusing that just a few months ago a funny thing happened to St. Christopher on his way to the altar! Here we are, celebrating a day on which everyone who has even the tiniest drop of Irish blood stands together, arm in arm, friends to the last. But it is a time in history so torn by riots, demonstrations, and campus takeovers that one politician calls it an age which prefers vice to virtue, protest to prayer, and whoopie to worship! Here we are, celebrating a day on which, by a kind of universal dispensation, everybody says kind things about the Irish. But it is a time in history so racked by the extreme exaltation of love that a cartoon in last month's *New Yorker* rings true. It shows two hippies animatedly conversing as one says to the other: "You know, I'm so far gone on love that I hate anybody who isn't."

Yet, are all the kind things people say about the Irish true? Or are Irish myths just so much blarney? This evening I would like to examine with you one such myth, the one that describes the Irish as a lighthearted, carefree, ebullient race. I have known Irish people since I was a child, but I've never seen evidence of the gaiety, lightheartedness, and alleged absence of melancholy of the children of St. Patrick.

Quite the contrary. It is surely a key to our true character that we made a national social institution out of wakes.

The French meet their relatives at weddings.

The Italians meet theirs at baptisms—eventually.

The Germans meet at banquets or beer fests.

The Yankees meet at bank directors' meetings.

And we Irish, we meet at wakes!

Sometimes it's the only place some Irish see most of their relatives; certainly it's the only place one ever sees his father's people!

All this lighthearted and unmelancholy spirit of the Irish seems less impressive when you reflect on the percentage of our jokes that are bound up with corpse-houses, wakes, and sudden death!

Then, too, we are the only people in the world who date everything from The Time of the Trouble.

The Jews, with one notable exception, date everything from the Creation of the World. The Romans date everything from the Foundation of the City. The English from 1066. Americans from 1492, 1620, 1776, or the Chicago Fire.

But we date things from The Trouble. We are the only people in the world who spell the word "trouble" with a capital "T."

But we are supposed to be the unmelancholy people, the lighthearted, merry people.

I don't find evidence of it. I don't, certainly, find it in the most typical of our songs, by which I mean, of course, our authentic songs, the songs of Old Ireland, not the ersatz ballads of Tin Pan Alley, the Comail.

Think for a moment of one of our most cherished ballads, "The Minstrel Boy." There's a lighthearted song for you!

The first question in your mind may be, "Where is he?" And the answer is "To the war he's gone."

You say, "I think I'll send him a card. Where is he posted?"

And the answer comes early in the song: "In the ranks of death you'll find him."

Other nationalities sing of eventually coming home, but not the Irish! In reality we have, of course, our full share of casualties, but many of our lads live to fight again. But not in our songs. In the songs no man ever survives, and none dies a natural death.

Think of that other lighthearted song, "Danny Boy."

She makes it plain that she doesn't expect ever to see him again. If by unlikely chance he comes back, however, she invites him to drop out to the cemetery, where she'll be lying cold and dead. "And I shall hear, though soft you tread above me."

That's light and cheerful; we Irish are really hilarious. "If I am dead, as dead I well may be."

It's a foregone conclusion that we never see an Irishman come back in our songs, but if he does, it's only to pay a visit to the graveyard.

Then there's that other lovely, lighthearted, merry song "Kathleen Mavourneen."

"Kathleen Mavourneen, the gray dawn is breaking."

Now the Italians sing about dawn. They call it *mattinata*, but it is always a rosy dawn for them, one worth getting up for.

"Kathleen Mavourneen." He wakes her up at crack of dawn—a gray dawn—to say good-bye.

When will he be back? "It may be for years—and it may be forever!"

It might be next Tuesday, but we never admit it in our songs! There's no *a bieniot!* or *arrividerci!* with us. It's for years—or forever!

We're a lighthearted people, indeed.

Our English cousins across the Irish Sea at present are charging a shilling a head to go in and see their old houses. They are desperately trying to pay the taxes on them. It's humiliating and sad. But they don't admit it. They sing about the "stately homes of England."

With us it's "The Tumble-down Shack in Athlone!" The roof is falling in, and everybody is gone to Australia—at least, according to the song.

Then we have a beautiful ballad about "The Harp That Once Through Tara's Halls." There's a cheerful song!

"Neglected hangs on Tara's walls, because its soul has fled!"

It's dead too! It's like the fellow out under the hill in "The Kerry Dancers." That music strikes up, and you think "This is going to be a little bit sprightly! This will relieve the evening a bit." But then in the last stanza you discover that all the dancers are dead! They used to be around, but now they're "gone, alas, like my youth, too soon!"

Some of the Irish did survive to get to America. They seem to be enjoying it pretty well, but, if we can believe the songs, they're just putting on a brave front. Secretly, they're heartbroken, dying to go back. They have a little song about that, too: "I'll Take You Home Again, Kathleen!"

In this cheerful song he promises to bring her "to where your heart has ever been!"

The chances are her heart's been in Macy's or Gimbel's for years, but that's not Irish music.

We have to pretend that she's heartsick for Ireland, and

the clear implication is that she's not going to make it; she's too sick to stand the trip!

So before she leaves, we sing her a cheerful, lighthearted song called, "Believe Me, If All Those Endearing Young Charms."

When the Italian sings to his girl friend, he tells her she is the loveliest thing in the spring. And even the English have courage to pay a compliment or two in their ditties. The French are, of course, geniuses at it.

But us: "Around the dear ruins!"

And for an encore we sing "The Last Rose of Summer"— "left blooming alone!"

We're a lighthearted lot, no doubt! Anyone who says different is indulging in anti-Irish propaganda!

Now don't misunderstand me: these songs are very beautiful, the most beautiful in the world. They are hauntingly beautiful, but they are not funny, or lighthearted, or merry.

"The great Gaels of Ireland are the men that God made mad; for all their wars are merry, and all their songs are sad!"

Is this lack of gaiety a bad thing? Is it a fault in our spirit? No! I think it is a positive contradiction to our times. We are not a carefree people. We feel deeply about the things that matter. As one wise man remarked, "For these three things we care: Our God, Our Country, and Our People—and we keep it quiet!" So in this world of glitter and show, let us keep our sobriety. Let us preserve our beautiful heritage in song and character. Let's join in the serenity of this old Irish blessing:

> "May the road rise to meet you,
> May the wind be always at your back,
> May the sun shine warm upon your face,
> May the rains fall soft upon your fields,
> And until we meet again, may the Lord hold
> you in the palm of His hand."

CHRISTMAS & EASTER

A CHRISTMAS SERMON

Christmas is a birthday, but not of Washington, or Jefferson, or Lincoln, or Lee. It is God's birthday as man. The most explosive sentence in the entire Bible is St. John's: "The Word became flesh and came to dwell among us." First a baby, this Jesus slowly grew into the boy who worked as an apprentice in the carpenter shop and then became the man who associated with fishermen, the God-Man who loved the underdog, who was all-merciful to sinners, and who loved the down-and-outers and the poor. Jesus said of himself, "The foxes have their holes and the birds have their nests, but the Son of Man has nowhere to rest his head."

How many today observe Christ's birthday, how few his precepts! Christmas, which once was a sacred feast, has become mostly a secular festival. It's easier to keep the holidays than to keep the Commandments.

Yet, if Christian asceticism were to take its cue from Sacred Scripture, there would surely be much more emphasis on the second coming of Christ, the end of time, when he will come in "power and glory." It is easy to think of Christ as a baby. It is disturbing to think of him as Judge and Lord of all human history.

The most volatile truth of Christianity is that simple fact. God entered into history, and history entered into God. Eternity entered into time and time was absorbed into eternity. The Christian calendar reflects this astounding fact of history with the simple abbreviations A.D. and B.C. Yet 1900 years have come and gone, and Jesus the Savior is still the central figure of our confused world society afflicted with an obsession for speaking out and an aversion for thinking through.

The theme of Bethlehem is peace on earth to persons of good will. Blessed are the peacemakers, because they shall be called the children of God. By our Baptism we Catholics are the Peace Corps of Christ. So the Prince of Peace chooses the rough boards of a cattle crib as his sacred cradle, and bypasses the war-lords, money-lords, and sex-lords of our society. In that cold cave there was a peace of mind that this world cannot give. There was also humility, obedience, poverty, and love.

This had to be, because Bethlehem was the first step on the long road to Calvary. Jesus journeyed from the horizontal life he experienced at birth to the vertical life at his death on the cross. Thus he told us that nobody in their right mind could claim that Christianity is supposed to be an easy religion. It requires a strong backbone. It is not a liberal, country-club, think-and-do-as-you-please, spiritual discotheque sort of thing, with drinks on the house. Perhaps that is why Christ, as he grew to manhood, would say, "If anyone wishes to come after me, let him take up his cross" . . . from the womb to the tomb.

Man as created by God is deeply rooted in space and time. He cannot turn back the hands of time nor can he turn them ahead. Ages ago St. Paul cried out to the Gentiles, "Now is the acceptable time for your salvation." This gives us a purpose for Christmas.

Life is not a cabaret, and Camelot is not in the real world. The love of power will threaten our power to love. Our Christmas ideal is essentially faith, hope, and charity. It is a vision leading to faith, a resignation leading to hope, and a compassion leading to charity.

The Lord of Christmas is not the harmless infant, but the Lord and Judge of all human history, the Savior who is the sign of better things to come. If we do not recognize Christ as such, then Advent's truths fall upon silent ears.

Then the rule of the world's tyrants is still unbroken.

Then the war-lords, the money-lords, and the sex-lords remain unscathed.

Then the powers of greed, hatred, and exploitation grip too many hearts. But Pope _____ still pleads for the Christian ideal of the first Christmas, peace on earth. He does this despite the winter of discontent, the rain, the darkness, and the loneliness of mankind. The Church can realistically do no more. The ultimate responsibility and the decisive choice is humanity's. Our Christmas night will be a silent night and an uneasy night, with so many godless nations around the globe. But we will keep in mind those most provocative words uttered by human lips, "Blessed are the peacemakers for they shall be called the children of God."

EASTER: THE ROOTS OF OUR FAITH, HOPE & CHARITY

A few years back the most famous name in literary circles was that of Alex Haley. His novel, *Roots*, topped the best seller list for months, and the TV movie took the Nielsen ratings by storm. It became the most widely viewed television production in history.

One episode that especially impressed me centered on the African ritual called "Madinka." This was the ritual of naming a child. On the eighth day after the birth of her child the mother took the infant in her arms and brought him or her out into the presence of the whole village. She held out the newborn child to the father, who promptly whispered into the baby's ear. What did he whisper? A carefully chosen name by which the child would be known for the rest of his or her life.

The religious significance of this first public event for the baby is fascinating. Every human being should be the first to know who he or she is! In whispering the name to his child, the father fulfills this important duty. The newborn child is the first to hear his or her own name. Because of the Madinka ritual, the baby is the first to know his or her identity.

It seems to me that the feast we celebrate this evening is also an important person-naming ritual. Madinka and Easter are strikingly similar.

By the one, we are called Jim, Mary or Ann, and by the other, we are called Christians. By the one, you and I receive our name in body and by the other, you and I receive our name in spirit.

By the one, our identity is recognized at birth, and by the other, our identity is recognized at the Resurrection.

Tonight we cry, "He is risen!" When St. Augustine calls us "Easter people," he is simply reaffirming a well-known fact. No doctrine is more central to the Christian faith than the resurrection. Through the annals of human history, a few men have been raised from the dead, but only one rose. Great men in their lives have done great things and to prove it there are the test tubes of science, the bridges of engineering, the masterpieces of art, and the armies of conquest. But when they came to die, all their great deeds stopped—dead! But the resurrection of Jesus Christ is a wonder precisely for this reason: he turned his tombstone into the cornerstone of Christianity. And this teaches us a trinity of faith, hope, and love.

First, faith. If Christ be not risen from the dead, our faith is in vain. Christianity literally puts all its eggs in one basket, the Easter basket. Easter assures us that life is an epic not of Paradise Lost but of Paradise Regained. The resurrection of Our Lord gives a heightened dimension to the belief of William Faulkner that man will not merely endure, man will prevail. Any interpretation of Christianity that is exclusively preoccupied with Good Friday distorts the meaning of Christ and the understanding of how the life of Christ is to be appropriated in the life of the Christian and the life of the Church.

All of us live between Christmas and Easter, and we must never forget Lent. At birth, death merely steps aside. The moment we are born we begin to die. And God sometimes makes us live in this world as if he did not exist, just as he allowed his own Son to be edged off this world and up onto a cross just two short days ago. Then the God-Man cried out, "My God, my God, why have you forsaken me?"

This is how our faith comes into play on Easter Sunday. All too often we resemble the disciples as well as the women of that first Easter morn, who seemed to remember the passion more than the resurrection, more the Good Friday than the Easter Sunday, more his suffering than his eternal joy. Like ourselves, they were the same mysterious mixture of death and life, despair and hope, pain and peace as they witnessed Christ pass through the tomb of many broken dreams to the glorious sunshine of the resurrection morn.

Second, hope. Easter Sunday puts everything about Jesus into perspective and tells us what Good Friday was all about. It gives us hope. It shows that what really happened on Good Friday was not a defeat but a triumph. We say that the story of every hero of history runs into a dead-end street with his demise. But this Jesus left no stone unturned, not even his tombstone, to prove that he is unique, that he is God and Savior. This is our hope for a better and eternal life.

Third, love. Many times in our spiritual lives we find that Jesus is elusive. Just when we think that we have him cornered, we lose him. We don't know where they put him. Perhaps we subconsciously echo the words of Mary Magdalene: "The Lord has been taken from us . . . we do not know where to find him." Modern day Christians often fail to recognize Christ in their midst among the starving, the indigent, the sick and the hungry. They want only the cushion of the comfortable Christ.

But Christ said, "Whatever you do to the least of my brothers, you do unto me."

Are we open to accepting this new life? Are we loving and compassionate to those around us? Are we aware of God revealing himself at this "special moment" of history? Karl Rahner says that man by his very nature "longs" to belong. Bernard Lonergan says that man possesses an "unrestricted eros" for total fullness of life.

This celebration of Christ's resurrection is an answer to our longing and insatiable thirst for happiness. Easter is God's magnanimous "yes" to all of us. The disciples believed this. They felt that when Jesus rose from the dead, God had said "yes" to Jesus. Just as the African father whispers that identifying name to his newborn son in the Madinka ritual, so our Father can whisper that "yes" to us as we cling to the newly risen Lord. This is the heart of the Easter message.

St. Paul says, "God loves a cheerful giver." Because of Easter, perhaps we should say, "God loves the cheerful life." Christians always put on a happy face, but for a solid reason. They get happiness, joy, hope, and meaning from the Easter Christ, who conquered the dark grave of death so that the last Station is no longer the end. The 14 Stations of the Cross are useless, are devoid of meaning, and make no sense unless we look at them from the perspective of the fifteenth Station, the Resurrection. That is what the empty grave of Christ tells the Christian. The difference between faith and no faith is the difference between bright hope and black despair, between shining happiness and a gloomy fate, between night and day, between here and hereafter. That is what Easter is all about. That is the cause, the meaning, and the roots of our joy today.

THE MEANING OF LENT

LENT—SAVIOR—SIN—SUFFERING

In the home of a well-known Philadelphia physician there hangs a remarkable picture. Remarkable because the subject—Jesus Christ—is depicted in twentieth century style. The artist has succeeded in placing our Lord in modern-day circumstances.

Jesus is seen sitting on a park bench, with the New York City skyline behind. All about him, children romp at their play. A young boy frantically chases a model airplane through the park. A small girl cuddles her talking doll at his feet. A group of youngsters are boisterously playing a game of baseball. Others leap and dance at their contest of following the leader.

But the focal point of the picture is Jesus. He is holding a small girl on his lap. The girl is obviously troubled. She has been examining our Lord's hand. Quizzically, she opens her mouth for a question. This question the artist has usurped for the title of his painting. The question, the title: "What happened to your hand?"

What happened to your hand? This evening, my dear friends, I would like to pose for your scrutiny another question. The season of Lent has once again come around in the Church's calendar. What has happened to it? What is the meaning of Lent for today's Catholic?

Casual observation and conversation indicate that Lent no longer means what it used to mean for many Catholics. The somewhat strict Church rules on fast and abstinence have been greatly modified. Many Catholics have also abandoned their former Lenten practices. After all, giving up desserts or alcohol does not seem to make a lot of difference in our contemporary world.

The proper starting place for reflection upon these questions is the meaning of Lent itself. Catholics have traditionally celebrated Lent as a time of penance and preparation for Easter. This Special Season has been in vogue since the fourth century. In fact, by the year 839 A.D., the standard 40 days of Lent was fixed for all Christendom as extending from Ash Wednesday through Holy Saturday.

It is noteworthy that the number 40 is itself often viewed as sacred. Forty is the number of days of the Flood; the number of years of the Israelites' wandering; the number of days of the fast of the prophet Elias; the number of days of grace given by Jonas in his preaching at Nineveh; the number of days Moses spent on Sinai; and, of course, the number of days Jesus fasted in the desert.

It is precisely from such a historical perspective that I again ask: "What has happened to the meaning of Lent?" Is there still a place for the reality of penance in contemporary Catholic life?

I think the answer to these questions is yes, and because of three factors. Three factors that give meaning to Lent for today's Catholic. Three factors that justify the importance of penance during the Special Forty Day Season we are now celebrating. Three factors that can be simply summed up as: Savior, Sin and Suffering.

The first factor that gives meaning to Lent for today's Catholic is Savior. Beyond any doubt the call to do penance occupies a central place in the Gospel of Jesus. Mark summarizes the entire teaching of Christ in this matter with the familiar words: "This is the time of fulfillment. The reign of God is at hand! Do penance and believe in the Gospel. Repent and be Saved!" (Mk 1:14). This call to penance, this cry for conversion, this challenge for a fundamental change of heart has constantly remained one of the most important biblical and Christian themes.

In the early Church, preaching constantly stressed the need for a joyful acceptance of Jesus, the need for the fundamental conversion. Penance is a most acceptable way of bringing about this death and new life. The very word "mortification" (a synonym for penance) tells us so. *Mors* and *ferre* are twin Latin words meaning death-bringing. And mortification is any practice of penance which causes death to sin. It is a virtue by which we deprive ourselves of what is lawful, in the hope that we may later resist what is unlawful.

Behold the necessity of mortification—the necessity of self-denial. St. Philip Neri said: "Where there is no mortification, there is no sanctity." The great St. Augustine echoes his words: "Lord, here on earth cut, here on earth burn—but spare me for Eternity!" These saints and our Lord certainly knew what they were talking about! For mortification removes the obstacles to grace, just as prayer does. In fact, mortification and prayer work hand in hand.

When the Jews were building the city of Jerusalem, they first erected huge walls that were to encircle their new home. Because of their many enemies, however, they were obliged to be constantly prepared for fighting, as well as for working. As a result, historians relate that the Jews worked with a trawl in one hand and a sword in the other. Spiritual authors tell us that we too, while building the spiritual walls that encompass our immortal soul, have need of a trawl in one hand, and a sword in the other: the trawl of prayer, and the sword of mortification.

The second factor that gives meaning to Lent for today's Catholic is Sin. Calvin Coolidge, the 30th president of the United States, was a regular church-going man. He was also a taciturn Vermonter. One Sunday he went to the Services as usual while his wife remained behind at home because of a cold. When Coolidge returned, his wife asked him what the sermon was about. "It was about sin," Calvin replied. "What did the preacher say about sin?" continued his wife. "Well," answered Coolidge, "he said that he was agin' it!"

Paradoxically, because some people seem to be "for" sin, instead of "agin" it, penance has value today. Call it conversion, call it penance, call it change of heart, this important Christian reality presupposes the existence of sin. This is why penance makes no sense apart from sin. It helps us to realize that for every sin we commit there is a price-tag of suffering and atonement that we must pay. Yet there are people who deny that sin exists.

Indifference to sin is nothing else but a spiritual disease of defective nerve endings. I maintain the difficulty people are experiencing with Lent and with penance arises from this indifference, this complacency, this lethargy. What about us? Do we have a proper understanding of our own sinfulness?

But an intellectual understanding of sin is not sufficient. I must become convinced of my own sinfulness, of the lack of love in my relations with God, neighbor and the world. We are usually reluctant, unwilling to admit our own continuing sinfulness. There is something disturbing about acknowledging our sinfulness. We are all tempted to play the role of the biblical Pharisee and thank God that we are not like the rest of men.

Lent means a time for reflecting, for comparing our lives with the gospel ideal. We need to be rudely shocked into the recognition of how far short of the Christian ideal we fall. Let those who are without sin say they have no need of penance or of Lent.

The third factor that gives meaning to Lent for today's Catholic is Suffering. Legend recounts that three trees once stood in a dense forest. They often wondered what would become of them when the woodsman cut them down. One day the trees decided to pray. Pray for what they wished to be when turned into lumber.

The first tree asked to become part of a beautiful palace. A palace where kings and queens might dwell. Where the great would come and gaze in amazement. The second tree asked to become part of a great ship that would sail the seven seas. A ship that would travel around the world. The third tree preferred to stay in the forest. It asked to grow into the tallest tree of all, and forever to point like a finger to God.

Sometime later, a woodsman came with saw and axe. Down went the first tree. But instead of being made into a beautiful palace, it was made part of a common stable. Yet, in that stable a Virgin Mother and her just husband took shelter on a certain night when a beautiful Baby was born. Ever since, kings and peasants, the great and the small, have honored that simple stable. They have echoed the song of the angels that Christmas night: "Glory to God in the highest, and on earth peace to men of good will."

Some years ago, Bishop Fulton J. Sheen made this statement: "Today's greatest tragedy is not that there is so much suffering in the world. It is rather that there is so much wasted suffering."

"Wasted Suffering!" An idea well worth pondering, my dear friends. When Oscar Wilde said that he could sympathize with everything except suffering, his readers probably found the wisecrack offensive and yet not wholly unaccountable. For suffering is too common to be interesting, too terrible to be taken for granted and too mysterious to be understood by human intelligence left to itself.

All this may seem like flashing lights around the obvious. Yet it is necessary to explain the paradox of suffering. On the one hand, pain is inevitable. It surrounds us. It will always be our lot. On the other hand, so much pain is wasted. So much is borne without merit. So much is spent without value. Why?

According to Pope Pius XI, suffering is the highest form of prayer. Father Faber calls it the greatest of the sacraments. Blessed Theophane compares it to the coin by which you and I purchase heaven. Why then the paradox? How can we explain the riddle of wasted suffering?

Why? How? The answer, my dear friends, can only be found on Calvary. For on Calvary stands the Cross. The Cross which epitomizes the meaning of Lent.

Whether we are young or old, married or single, my dear friends, of this we can be sure. With all our suffering, you and I are today nailed either on the right of Christ's Cross or on the left. What determines our position? Only our answer to the paradox of suffering.

Here, then are three factors which, in my opinion, give meaning to Lent in the life of today's Catholic—Savior, Sin and Suffering. As we conclude, I ask you to think back to that little girl sitting on Christ's lap. That day she discovered the scars of Jesus. Today we have once again arrived at this realization.

If Jesus Christ, our leader, wore scars—then surely we, his soldiers, must be prepared on the day of the great review. Prepared to show him the scars we have worn in his cause. That to each of us, Jesus will say "What happened to your hands?" Woe to that Christian who steps forward with hands unscarred and white! Woe to that Christian who steps forward unmindful of his sinfulness to God and neighbor! Woe to that Christian who steps forward to place his cross of suffering at Christ's left hand!

Part III

Occasional Addresses

This section consists of many of Fr. McNulty's formal retreat addresses which have been edited to meet the need for briefer homilies. It also includes scripts of taped cassettes he recorded over the years with Alba House Publications. They too have been edited for better readability.

JESUS CHRIST—SAVIOR OR SUPERSTAR

Recently, psychologist Eugene Kennedy was interviewed about his attendance at the Jesus People Convention at Notre Dame. His reactions were most uncomplimentary.

"It was a scary experience," said Kennedy. "The participants had everything on the floor except sawdust. While the proceedings were full of emotion, I got no sense of genuineness. There was manipulation, not unlike that used by Hitler or Mussolini. The assemblage was muttering stuff that was supposed to be prayers, but the only other place I have heard that sound, where the tone rises, is in mental hospitals at night when something has disturbed the patients. I almost expected someone to give Jesus a standing ovation by saying: 'give me a J . . . give me an E . . .' In short, if this experience is religious, count me out. It is not religion, it is hysteria."

I don't know that I agree with Eugene Kennedy's rather violent reaction to the Jesus Movement. There is no denying the fact that Jesus is exploding into our contemporary scene in an apocalypse of sight and sound undreamed of even five years ago. Jesus plays are on Broadway. Jesus songs are popular on radio stations. There are Jesus sweatshirts, buttons and even bikinis. These are inundating our country, our culture, our consciousness.

Isn't it very true? Last Christmas, you could give someone you love, a gift which could put him "with Jesus every minute of the day." It was a "Jesus watch" and it sold for $19.95. In the words of the advertiser, "Our Jesus watch comes with the Savior's likeness, in the race of your choice, complete with an ever-revolving crimson heart." The businessmen responsible for the Jesus watch, it is reported, got their inspiration from a rubber squeaking Buddha doll.

Outrageous? Not if you make your living on Madison Avenue. Jesus has become such a folk hero, and such a social phenomenon in the seventies, that American merchandising has accorded Him a place in our pop culture alongside Mickey Mouse and Spiro Agnew. In fact, you may remember that five years ago John Lennon, the most outspoken of the Beatles, tossed off a remark that his singing group was more popular than Jesus. Critics blasted him for glib irreverence, but he was probably speaking the truth. Ironically, today the Beatles no longer exist, and Jesus is characterized as a Superstar.

As Christians, we grew up in an era when the proclaimers of Jesus were the churches. Can today's pop culture and the wire services really transmit the message of the Jesus phenomenon? In short, as Christians, we were very concerned about proclaiming Jesus as a Savior. Should we be cynical then about his meteoric transformation as a Superstar?

What am I saying? Simply this. We can judge if Jesus is alive in terms of what we create all around ourselves. There are some people today who call themselves Christians, yet all around them is dismay, neurotic anxiety, constant self-defense and all sorts of discord. For some of them, what is happening in their church is too little, too late, too slow, too burdensome, too filled with tensions and struggles. Hung up on future forms of ministry, future kinds of life styles, future ideas of commitment. They refuse to live in the present where Jesus is.

There are still others in the church who believe what is happening is too drastic, too fraught with insecurity, too worldly, too free, too unstructured. They believe there is no need for any major changes, or at least for the degree to which these changes are occurring. Hung up on an inadequate theology of the Pilgrim church, of heaven being more imminent than life's needs, they too refuse to live in the present where Jesus is.

The excruciating pity of all this is that for both groups, the church has become a life about Jesus, rather than a life with Jesus. I know Jesus is here when I meet someone in whose presence I receive hope. Someone who convinces me by his life style, that peace has a better chance in the world. Someone who is intent on fostering reconciliation with his fellow man.

Reconciliation! Maybe this is the crux of the matter. The crux of whether Jesus is Life for you and for you and for me. Beyond any doubt, the present decade is anything but a decade of reconciliation. Rather it can be described as a decade of divisions. Some words have become charged and bitter, like "hippie," "establishment," "institutional church," "thirty." Old words have taken on new meanings: "marches" no longer mean parades, "demonstrations" no longer mean free advertising, "Panthers" no longer mean lions and tigers in Africa. Now in the seventies, hair has become longer, pants and skirts shorter. Yet in the religious life, there are still clusters of adolescent camps. Camps that are poles apart in respect for personal choice, for responsible freedom, for openness to the needs of all God's children.

This is indeed incredible arrogance. Anyone who is clustered in one of those camps doesn't have the life of Christ in him because Christ doesn't come to a camp or a club. He comes to people.

Christianity gambles recklessly to turn out the very best we can hope for. Sartre insists there is no exit. Christianity maintains there are exits everywhere. Sartre would ask what has the world come to? Christianity asks what has come to the world? Sartre says hell is other people. Christ says that if we go to hell, we go there over his dead body. This is no country club religion.

Why? Because Christianity alone of all religions, has the audacity to affirm this basic hope which the world represses. Jesus was the baffling contradiction who inverted the order from power to love. This brought about a new order of society. A new philosophy of history and a new destiny for humanity. A new sense of God.

It is fantastically important for us to see Jesus in the garbage of our day to day existence. Why? Because the future of our contemporary society lives in the hands of those who are strong to provide reasons for living and hoping. We need vision. The vision of God that we may see Jesus in our daily existence. To see Jesus the Savior making the difference in the terms of our lives. To see Jesus giving us the inspiration to live more fully, more hopefully and more peacefully so that when the words of Christ are reiterated, "Who do you say I am?", we can say, as the children of God, "You are Jesus, You are love, you are life, you are our Savior."

RECONCILIATION

Some years ago, two films from Hollywood succeeded in luring large numbers of Americans to the theatre. Both dealt with violence. I am speaking of "Death Wish" and "California Split." Starring brawny Charles Bronson, "Death Wish" was about external violence—crime in the streets. Bronson became a one-man vigilante committee. "California Split" dealt with internal or psychic violence, a key symptom of the modern, confused person who lacerates relatives and friends because of the frustration and acute loneliness he or she carries within.

Whatever its source, violence today is a harsh reality that speaks loudly and clearly, not of reconciliation, but of the alienation and estrangement of countless people. This alienation exists between people and nature, between the individual and self, and between people everywhere. The fallout from these three separations affects us all profoundly. Let us briefly analyze this phenomenon and then offer ideas that may bring about reconciliation.

Alienation between people and nature. The late Erich Fromm, a psychoanalyst, once said he was extremely gloomy about the future of America. He said our incredible excess of material things has "minified" people and made life seem unimportant to them. We have abandoned our goal of dominating nature and, paradoxically, this has been reversed with the threat of ecological disaster haunting us.

Many of us take nature for granted. Nothing on earth or in the sea or sky can resist American ingenuity. One tradition even boasted that our consistent success and material prosperity was a sign of God's election. America was the chosen land. Today this has suddenly changed. The land, the air, the wealth we have, all threaten to destroy us. There is the recurring joke, "When does the snow get dirty in New York City? At 10,000 feet." Each year Americans junk seven million cars, 48 billion cans, and 20 million tons of paper; they belch 172 million tons of fumes into the sky, and no end is in sight.

These facts and figures are frightening, and they indicate how we are enlarging the alienation between people and nature. They call to mind the curse of God in Genesis, "Cursed is the ground because of you." We have fashioned a monster out of God's earth and now the monster threatens to destroy us. This hostility between people and their environment is parallel to people and their sense of sin today; both are reaching the point of no return.

The alienation between people and nature helps us escape reality. Last year in the United States over 8 billion tranquilizers were sold; this means each person would have enough for two months. "If your environment causes you stress, take an Alka Seltzer." "We helped you in the thirties and we can do it again in the seventies—take an aspirin." Perhaps instead of sipping a Scotch or popping a pill, we should follow the advice of St. Paul, "Be faithful to yourself and your goals in Jesus Christ." Then we will realize that God did not intend us to be despots over nature, but rather responsible stewards of it.

Alienation between the individual and self. This springs from the individual. It is an identity crisis that confuses and confounds, torments and detracts, unglues and unhinges. We're something like the patient in the New York psychiatrist's office who yelled "We're here because we're not all there."

Human history manifests different states. First came the primitive, nomadic society, which involved survival of the fittest. Then followed the primitive identity society when man became agrarian, preserved food, and became involved with his fellow man. Individuals cooperated for the good of all. Then came the civilized society. Life became organized.

Living space became a priority. Power became a hallmark, and wars were waged over land. Work became for many sacrifice, not fulfillment. Finally, about 1950, humankind turned another corner. The individual returned to seeking self-fulfillment. Personal satisfaction and involvement became important once again. An entire generation grew up in affluence, not depression. People wanted gratification and achievement, which brings tension and contradiction. The individual and self suffer schizophrenic alienation. The person out of touch with self is out of touch with God. A year ago the bishops of the United States stated, "Such an outlook of our society overlooks the source of man's dignity and the fact that he is made in the image and likeness of God."

Reconciliation between the individual and self can only come about when one says, "I am who I am," accepting the self completely, talents and faults together, not up with the angels, but not down in the gutter either. After all, we were called by St. Paul to be "the children of God," and that is why Augustine said, "Our hearts are restless until they rest in you."

Alienation among individuals. People can be insanely cruel to one another . . . from the human ashes in Dachau to the living corpses in Calcutta . . . to the words of hate in suburban New York . . . two world wars . . . to the bombs . . . napalm converting Vietnam into a ghastly incinerator. Each night two out of every five persons on our planet go to bed hungry. The North Atlantic nations, with 16% of the world's population, control 80% of the world's wealth.

This alienation among individuals is a contemporary legacy of Cain. For us, it is not out there but in here, within you and me. They should know we are Christians by our love. We should not forget that God loves our whole being. Reconciliation comes when we see and fulfill the needs of others, be it affection, security, achievement, or self-worth. It really means that we have to care. And if we care, that will cure the alienation between individuals. As Christ said, "Whatsoever you do for the least of my brethren, you do for me."

I have spoken of reconciliation as it pertains first to people and nature, second to the individual and self, and third to the individual and others. We began by talking about violence in the films "Death Wish" and "California Split," a violence symptomatic of alienation. I conclude with words symptomatic of reconciliation, words of truth, words of depth, words worth carrying in our hearts and souls:

"Unless you become as little children, you shall not enter the kingdom of heaven."

MARRIAGE

In the sardonic musical, "Stop the World—I Want to Get Off!" the anti-hero sings: "What kind of fool am I? Who never fell in love. It seems that I'm the only one I'm thinking of. What kind of man is this? An empty shell. A lonely cell in which an empty heart must dwell. What kind of clown am I? What do I know of life? Why can't I cast away the mask of play and live my life? Why can't I fall in love, like any other man? Maybe then I'll know, what kind of fool I am."

The characterization of the human person as a fool is commonplace in literature. In the Old Testament the psalmist points out that "the fool says in his heart there is no God." In the New Testament, Christ speaks of five wise virgins and five foolish virgins. In Shakespeare's "A Midsummer Night's Dream" Puck exclaims, "Lord, what fools these mortals be!" And a popular song tells us that "Fools rush in where angels fear to tread."

When you get married you do a very foolish thing. In this humdrum age of planned obsolescence, shifting values, fluid commitments, vanishing absolutes, and changing loyalties, you pledge yourselves to each other for life. You promise to be faithful to each other in good times and in bad, in sickness and in health, until death. Do you realize what a risk you are taking?

You place yourselves in each other's hands. You are completely vulnerable to another person. With that person and with your children, you are risking your whole future in the gamble that it will bring you happiness, enrich your lives, and ultimately lead you to a blessed eternity. Why do you take that risk? Why, in spite of so many other more carefree life styles which society offers you today, do you choose marriage?

You could choose the more tranquil life of the person who lives alone with fewer demands, fewer requirements, fewer heartaches, and fewer headaches. Or you could choose one of the many options of living together that our contemporary society presents to us. The communes are available, and arrangements of simply living together for a temporary period of time also can be attractive to some people.

But you have chosen marriage, and you've not chosen simply a civil ceremony but a marriage in the Christian tradition. In a Catholic marriage, you pledge yourselves to each other not only before the community, your families and friends, but before Almighty God. You do this because you know that:

Marriage is not a merry-go-round in which you jump on until the music stops playing.

Marriage is not a spiritual smorgasbord where you pick and choose until you are filled.

Marriage is not a league for spiritual discovery where you tune in and then drop out.

Accordingly, you are about to enter into a union that is most sacred and most serious. It is most sacred because it is established by God himself and because it will bind you together for life in a relationship so close and so intimate that it will profoundly influence your whole future.

That future, with its hopes and disappointments, its successes and its failures, its pleasures and its pains, its joys and its sorrows, is hidden from your eyes. You know that these elements are mingled in every life and are to be expected in your own.

Truly, these words are most serious. It is a beautiful tribute to your undoubted faith in each other that, recognizing their full import, you are nevertheless so willing and ready to pronounce them. Henceforth, you belong entirely to each other, you will be one in mind, one in heart, and one in affections. Whatever sacrifices you may hereafter be required to make to preserve this common life, always make them generously. Sacrifice is usually difficult and irksome. Only love can make it easy, and perfect love can make it a joy.

Today at this rite, you say to each other, "I give myself to you. I give myself to you alone, and finally, I give myself to you always. Not until we have a fight, or until we have a problem, or until things get difficult, but until always." This lifelong commitment is one of the major characteristics of Christian marriage.

To think that this marriage will be totally free of suffering and difficulty, trials and traumas, is foolish. We are a mysterious mixture of death and life, despair and hope, pain and peace, good and bad. Just as Christ had to suffer and die before he rose from the dead, so every marriage will have its times of crucifixion as well as its times of resurrection. Don't forget, the uncomfortable Good Friday did come before the bouncy alleluias of Easter Sunday.

Why, then, do you take the foolish risk today? Basically it is a question of faith. You have faith in each other and in God. In this faith, which is rooted in the firm Christian foundation of trust and love, you find that the risk of Christian marriage is not foolish at all. In the light of God's love for us, it is perhaps one of the sanest and most sensible risks a man and a woman can take.

And so you pledge to each other today, with confidence, joy, and happiness. May this love with which you join your hands and hearts today never fail, but grow deeper and stronger as the years go on. The Christian community stands with you, filled with good hopes and wishes for you. And as we pledge to strengthen you by our prayers and our example, may God bless you and bring you joy and happiness through all the years of your married life.

THE CALL TO PARENTING

"I, a prisoner in the Lord, beseech you that you walk worthily of the vocation in which you are called."

(Ephesians 4:1)

I do not make a habit of reading the syndicated columns that give advice, but recently my sister sent me a clipping from just such a column. It provides a startling introduction to our topic for tonight, your vocation of parenting.

The clipping begins, "Dear Abby: The story of my life would make a good book. When I was 15, I married a man I hardly knew just to get out of the house. He turned out to be wanted by the police so I went home after 6 weeks. I was married again when I was 18 to a guy I thought that I loved. He was so drunk at our wedding, my father had to hold him up. . . . He drank like a fish so I got rid of him. Now I am going with another man. He is 14 years older than me and was married twice and has seven kids altogether. I think this is the one for me. But Abby, I hate to take a chance on three divorces before I'm 20. Should I marry him? He has to know before Wednesday. Signed, Cherie."

Here is Abby's answer: "Dear Cherie: Don't marry any man whose warranty runs out after Wednesday. If he's any good, he will keep. Two strikes is bad score, young lady, so don't swing again until it's a cinch."

This story, my dear women, is pitiful. Here is a young girl, not even 20, worrying about her third divorce. Here is a young person certainly in need of instruction on the most important element of her life: her vocation.

The vocation of marriage does not end with husband and wife. As Bishop Sheen has said: "A woman loves a man, and this love takes on a third dimension . . . This third dimension is called a child." And with the child, the married couple assumes the joys and responsibilities of parenting.

The challenge of Christian parenting is indeed exciting. About six months ago, a distinguished family expert published a book for parents entitled, *What to Do Until the Psychiatrist Comes*. A facetious title, yes, but many a mother today often wishes she were a trained psychiatrist. Trained that she might better understand the baffling period of life between childhood and adulthood, that period of life in which a youth bubbles and fizzles, that period of life which we adults classify as the bewildering teens.

Statistics paint a morbid picture for parents of today: one out of every 18 children is or will be a juvenile delinquent; one out of every 20 will end up in a mental institution; one out of every 50 will be a chronic alcoholic; seven out of every 10,000 are committing suicide every year; and 47% of those under 25 years of age are part of the age of dissent, the age of the critic, the age where to be in you have to be far out.

Why? One reason appears to be the growing tendency for parents to leave young people too much on their own and to grant the young unbridled freedom.

Do not misunderstand me. I am not saying that parents do not take a deep interest in their children. They do, but in many cases their interest is more in the physical than in the spiritual.

Many parents are more concerned about vitamins than virtue. Many are more concerned about children's carrots than character. Many are prompt to see that nothing harmful is put on the table at home but forget the poison these young people might imbibe once the front door is gleefully slammed. Parents often forget the four big W's: 1) Who their children's companions are; 2) What they intend to do; 3) Where they plan to go; 4) When they plan to return. For some parents these are minor matters—until tragedy strikes.

When tragedy does strike, parents sometimes scream in rage. But let me tell you what we have forgotten in such tragedies. Forgotten are the parents who didn't care enough to supervise their children's comings and goings. Forgotten are the adults who made a fat profit from selling liquor, a fat profit from drug traffic, a fat profit from the pornographic trade and the booking of immoral movies. Every one of these evils was conceived and operated by an adult. And where are the parents all this time? The parents who should have tried to take measures against these evils?

Raising good children is difficult, but many parents are doing it through proper parental guidance, and not the kind of guidance given by a mother I read about recently who gave a champagne party for her 11-year-old son in Garden City, New York. She said later, "How cute they were . . . they were all drunk."

It takes a double struggle for a mother to become a saint: sacrifice and good example. A philosopher of old spoke a great truth: the morality of the world depends upon its women. But we can go further and add that the morality of the family depends upon its mothers. Think back for a minute, my dear mothers, back to the greatest day in your life when you first held the bundle of warm, quivering flesh in your arms. Your first baby! How happy you were that day! What promises you made to God! What resolutions you formed about raising that wonderful child! Have you been faithful to these promises?

Remember your child knew you before he knew God; in fact, to your child you *were* God. Remember to keep him close to God by your good example, your continuous sacrifice, and the fulfilling of your Christian vocation to parenthood.

So tonight let me conclude by repeating those provocative words of the dynamic Apostle Paul:

"I, a prisoner in the Lord, beseech you that you walk worthily of the vocation in which you are called."

LOOKING AT AMERICA—
WITH HOPE OR HOPELESSNESS?

Recently I read the sad story of a priest who committed suicide. He had worked with blacks in the ghetto of South Bend, Indiana, and had worked hard, 12 and 14 hours a day, 365 days a year. He never took a vacation. After two years, the priest began wondering if what he was doing was really worthwhile. The poor were still poor. Society still seemed to be insensitive to his people's needs. The poor themselves still seemed unable to help themselves. So the priest felt he had failed. He became depressed and finally decided to commit suicide.

But not a "normal" kind of suicide—by gun, a knife, a rope, or pills. He wanted to kill himself in a very painful way so that by his suffering he could expiate his failure with his people. And so one morning he went into the kitchen of his rectory. From under the sink, he took a can of liquid Drano and drank it.

This terrible story dramatizes a spirit that seems to pervade America today, a spirit characterized by hopelessness, frustration, and alienation. A spirit epitomized by events like Kent State, Attica, Wounded Knee, Watergate, and Koreagate. A spirit highlighted by questions like "Why is it that with all our poverty programs, there are still millions of poor people in affluent America? Why is it that with all our leadership knowhow, planning resources, and scientific advances, this country seems to hurdle from one crisis to another?"

This spirit of hopelessness seems at first glance to be well-founded. Look at our government, for instance. Many Americans are disenchanted with our leadership today.

Whenever you mention Watergate or the Election Committee's bag of dirty tricks, whenever you allude to the possible impeachment of President Nixon or the forced resignation of our Vice President, whenever you speak of the energy crisis, coal strike, or inflation, people seem to have lost heart with the government. They are disappointed, alienated, lacking in hope.

What is true in government circles is also true of our Church. One critic has said that our Church today is the taillight of society, not the headlight. Another has remarked that institutional religion is looking at society in a rearview mirror, coming on the scene late as usual, to proclaim breathlessly the fact of what has gone wrong in the past. Attendance at liturgy is drastically down; so are vocations to the ministry. In fact, many priests, ministers, and rabbis have left their vocations. Religious institutions such as schools, hospitals, and social service centers seem to be in deep trouble. Few listen to Church leaders anymore. A deep credibility gap exists. Apparently people feel a hopelessness about where our Church is going.

So wherever we look, whether it be the government, church, or society, there do seem to be adequate grounds across this country for a sense of hopelessness and alienation.

But is America really sick? Can we say nothing positive about our nation?

Daniel Boorstin, Director of the Smithsonian Institute in Washington, affirms America's healthy spirit. As a matter of fact, he suggests that many of our national ills are imaginary, that many of them are not as serious as they appear, that too many Americans are guilty of being what Pope John called "prophets of doom."

Flooded by alarming headlines and televised news, melodramas of dissent and revolution, we torment ourselves with the illusory ideal of some "whole nation" that has a deep and outspoken faith in its values.

We become so obsessed by where we are that we forget where we came from and how we got here. No wonder we begin to lack the courage to confront the normal ills of modern history's most diverse, growing nation of nations. No wonder we face the present with hopelessness. We have lost our sense of history.

As Americans, you and I need to revive that sense of history. We need to hear again those magnificent voices from the past:

"I regret I have but one life to give for my country!"

"Don't give up the ship!"

"Damn the torpedoes! Full speed ahead!"

"I've come from Alabama with a banjo on my knee!"

"Pike's Peak or bust!"

"Give me liberty or give me death!"

"With malice towards none, with charity for all!"

I reiterate that, as Americans, you and I need to revive our sense of history. We need to reflect often on the rights and obligations of our citizenship. We need to recall the right to go to any church or synagogue we choose, or not to worship at all, as well as the obligation to respect others in the same light. We need to remember our right to harangue on a street corner, to hire a hall and shout our opinion until our tonsils are worn to a frazzle, and the obligation to curb our tongue now and then. We need to value anew the right to go to school, learn a trade, enter a profession, earn an honest living, and the obligation to do an honest day's work.

Yes, we Americans need to revive our sense of history. Too many people are caught up in the national hypochondria of the present moment. Knocking America has become a favorite pastime. Reviving the sense of our past achievements can answer this country's critics. It can take away the Drano from the hands of the hopeless. It can point out that the real cure lies not in emphasizing what's wrong with America, but rather what's right with America.

It was my good fortune to spend a few weeks in Israel. I found it a vital country, a blooming garden in the desert of the Middle East. One of the places in Israel that impressed me the most was the Sea of Galilee. This sea is very much alive. Fish swim in it. Children play on its banks. Birds build their nests near it. Everyone is happy that the Sea of Galilee is here. Lying south of the Sea of Galilee is a second sea. It, too, is fashioned by the flow of the River Jordan. But here things are different. No fish splash, no leaves flutter down, no birds sing, no children laugh. Here the traveler seldom passes and the air hangs heavy. Here neither man, nor beast, nor fowl stops to drink. For this sea is full of salt, decay, and stagnation. It is the Dead Sea.

The Sea of Galilee. The Sea of the Dead. What causes the mighty difference between these two neighboring bodies of water? Not the Jordan River, for this river empties the same good water into both. Not the soil in which the seas lie, for it is the same. Not the country or climate about, for both lie in Palestine.

The difference is this. For every drop of water it takes from the Jordan River, the Sea of Galilee gives up another drop. The Dead Sea, on the other hand, is a miser. It hoards its water. Thus, instead of giving life, it exudes sterility and decay.

I think the moral is obvious. There well may be two Americas today. The first is extrovertive, mindful of history, seeing everything in proper perspective; it is full of hope, inspiration and courage. The second is introspective, tied up only with the present, and full of hopelessness, decay, and alienation. To which America do you belong?

Christopher Columbus discovered America. You and I

must save America. We must revive America's history. For only by reviving the historical past can our country's present truly be seen as a period of hope, confidence, and greatness. Will we do this? As Americans, you and I are blessed to be part of a country with a glorious past, a challenging present, and a promising future.

May God bless America! May we save America!

THE AMERICAN CATHOLIC

Neil Simon's hit, "The Sunshine Boys," starring Jack Albertson and Sam Levine in its original Broadway production and George Burns and Walter Matthau in the motion picture version, is one of the funniest shows in years.

The heroes of "The Sunshine Boys," Willie Clark and Al Lewis, are retired vaudeville comedians. They have worked together on the stage as a team for forty years. As the show opens, NBC television is filming an hour-long special on "The History of Comedy." Willie and Al are invited to appear in one of their most famous skits. But unknown to NBC, these two men have not spoken to each other for years. Even while acting together and making everyone laugh, they were bitter enemies. The plot involves trying to reconcile these two comedians. Their moves to mate and checkmate each other make Bobby Fischer's prowess pale into oblivion. It is precisely their antics and gyrations that make "The Sunshine Boys" a very funny show and movie.

The similarity between these two aging comedians who present one face on stage and another off, and the terrifying ambiguity surrounding our double identity as Catholics and as Americans is compelling.

On the one hand, if anyone were to ask, "Can you be loyal both to your church and your country?", our unhesitating reply would be, "Yes, of course. I find no conflict between being Catholic and being American." John Kennedy answered this question during his 1960 presidential campaign. Even before that, you and I, as average American Catholics, simply did not believe that our government would ever do anything opposed to our faith. So we bedecked our churches with Old Glory, thus symbolizing our conviction that in the United States, God and country always stand together. Faith and patriotic obedience, if not the same, are at least complementary virtues. Good Catholics have to be good Americans.

On the other hand, America today seems to be moving against some of Catholicism's basic beliefs. Consider the law banning prayer in our public schools. Witness the movement to promote the homosexual life style. Think about the numerous court verdicts upholding pornography. Reflect upon the Supreme Court decision legalizing abortion on demand. In 1968 our bishops responded to this decision with vehemence: "The Supreme Court has declared that the unborn child is not a person in the terms of the Fourteenth Amendment. We reject this decision. Its orders completely lack judicial force. No one is obliged to obey this civil law."

When before in the history of the American church has the leadership of American Catholics proclaimed, "We shall not serve!"?

It all sounds like some story of another land and a beleaguered church fighting for its life against a hostile government. But it isn't. The scene is not Moscow or Santiago or Beirut. It's Washington. And that is what makes our double identity as Americans and as Catholics so ambiguous. Unlike the theatrical antics of Neil Simon's "The Sunshine Boys," this real life ambiguity is not laughable. It is tragic.

Harvey Cox, the Protestant theologian, recently made an interesting observation about the three major forms of religion prevalent in contemporary America. He distinguishes the three forms that religion takes: church religion, folk religion, civil religion.

Church religion is the kind symbolized by our churches and synagogues. It has a visible institutional form, buildings, staff, budget, and so forth. According to recent membership surveys, it is today in a period of decline.

Folk religion is the kind of rough and ready, hard to classify type of religions, expressions, and beliefs that people live by from day to day. This is the religious equivalent of folk culture or popular music. Religion without benefit of clergy, you might say.

Civil religion is the third form, and the one that here interests us the most. By this term, Cox means that religion peculiar to the American people in which the heroes, myths, and stories are identified religiously with the Pilgrim Fathers, with George Washington, and with heroes of various wars. This is the religion celebrated along the Potomac in the temples of Abraham Lincoln and Thomas Jefferson, the religion linking our inauguration rites, our national holidays, and our public banquets with a belief in law and order.

In America this system of meaning and value is alternatively called the civil religion, the secular religion, the "American way of life," or simply Americanism. Unfortunately, this set of values often spills over into our church religion, making us more American than Catholic.

It seems to me that we have gone back and forth in the deification of our leaders and in the degrees of loyalty to the civil religion. At times, from the point of view of Biblical faith, we have bordered on the sin of idolatry. We have been more American than Catholic.

How many American Catholics strive to imitate the ideals and life styles of both Horatio Alger and Jesus Christ? How many of us proclaim, "Every man for himself!" "Unlimited profit!" "Be Number One," and at the same time, "Be your brother's keeper"; "Blessed are the poor in spirit"; "The last shall be first." How many of us see no contradiction in these two world views?

Perhaps now that American Catholics have won middle class status, they believe that an unwritten rule of middle class status is not to rock the boat, not to challenge American values with Christian witness, not to really practice the faith we profess when the issues become uncomfortable.

Civil religion has been a fact of life in the United States for a long time. It surely will not die an easy death. But Vietnam and federal aid to abortion have struck it a serious blow. "Render to Caesar the things that are Caesar's," said Jesus. But Jesus is calling for civic loyalty, not religious loyalty, and that religious loyalty to Christ must take precedence over any other loyalty. Indeed, it might have to openly challenge another loyalty. For us Catholics the Gospel dream comes before the American dream.

Think back to George Burns and Walter Matthau in "The Sunshine Boys." Their ambiguous behavior is outrageously funny. Yours and mine are not. In fact, our ambiguous behavior could be tragic. Indeed, God and country may yet bed down together. But things will never be cozy again. How do we in the United States characterize ourselves? Are we American Catholics? Or Catholic Americans?

THE CATHOLIC AMERICAN

Recently an author seized upon the cowboy as the central figure in our American myth. In his book he compared the characteristics of cowboys and Indians in the Old West. His aim was to demonstrate that the cowboy, whom we all revered as yesterday's hero, was really today's villain and that the Indian, whom we all despised as yesterday's villain, is in reality today's hero. His analysis is fascinating.

The cowboy is first of all a loner, a Lone Ranger, a rugged individualist in the model of Teddy "Rough Rider" Roosevelt, while the Indian is a tribal person, a member of a collective commune, a family man. The cowboy is a hero, and he is self-aggrandized; the Indian aggrandizes the group. The cowboy has no roots, is always moving on into the sunset, and has no lasting relationships, no commitments. The Indian takes his identity from his tribal roots, from the tradition of his ancestors, and from the hope of offspring. The cowboy is restrained, bashful and introverted. The Indian is excitable and ecstatic; he gestures, and he dances.

The cowboy is a sexual puritan. He never kisses a girl. He might be asexual. The Indian is polygamous. Hollywood hints that he is sexually erratic and wild. The cowboy is aggressively violent; he prizes violent conflict. The Indian is defensively violent. He stands and fights with courage, but he does not seek war. The cowboy has the power, and he has a gun. The Indian has less power, and he holds the bow and arrow.

The author concludes by listing the qualities that make the Indian America's real hero. These qualities stand for many of the things you and I seek today. They are awe, silence, togetherness, wonder, communion, stillness. These are the gifts of the Indian. Violence, loneliness, restlessness, lack of commitment are not. These are the gifts of the cowboy.

It seems to me that the parallel between cowboys and Indians can easily be applied to today's American trying to *live his religious beliefs*. Why? Because today's American is a product of the twin forces of Protestantism and Catholicism. Due to their separate histories, each religion has developed different sides in their understanding of man and society. Like the cowboy, Protestantism has emphasized the individual. Like the Indian, Catholicism has emphasized community. Without declaring the one as the hero and the other as the villain, many Americans are now coming to see the danger of this cultural one-sidedness. Maybe the Catholic American has really been a Protestant American.

Consider for example, three specific areas in America's life style. All three are the legacy of Protestantism:

First is *hard work*. The Protestant work-ethic-run-wild has resulted in personal as well as national tragedy. The "workaholic" has become a cultural stereotype. Many families suffer because their fathers are only happy when they are working and feel guilty and purposeless when taking time out for relaxation and family recreation.

Second is *individual success*. Success in America is viewed as a long, lonely, uphill struggle. For many men, and an increasing number of women, moving up in the world of business means traveling more and spending less time with spouse and family. How many American families experience the loneliness reported by some families of International Business Machine employees for whom IBM has come to mean "I've Been Moved"? The pursuit of individual success has made us a nation of nomads.

Third is *guilt*. We feel guilty about so many things; our failures as parents, as children, as persons unable to be all we should be, to do all we should do. We think we should be perfect. When we aren't, we are either too afraid to admit our failure, or we indulge in self-hatred. When others fail, we turn on them with self-righteous moralizing: poor people are lazy, Southerners are racist, politicians are corrupt.

Today's Americans are dissatisfied with the results of this one-sided emphasis upon our heritage. They are searching for alternative values. Can we as Catholics offer viable solutions? Can we as Catholics proffer visions that could prove beneficial to American culture? Can we as Catholics temper work with leisure, loneliness with community, and guilt with forgiveness?

Consider our heritage of leisure. Someone has said that if America is a Protestant dream, California is a Catholic dream.

His thinking is that in California and the whole Southwest in general, the emphasis is on leisure, on the glories of sea and surf, of vineyard and siesta. This slower-paced life is really a hangover from the days when Spanish Catholics planted the early seeds of culture in America. Has it been forgotten in our country's apotheosizing of the "work ethic"?

Catholicism's answer to the Protestant legacy of guilt is forgiveness. Soren Kierkegaard, the famed existentialist, once remarked that the American way of life often leads to what he calls "despair of possibilities." The American creed is that an individual can do anything if he tries hard enough. He is a creature with no limits. Thus man ignores his limitations and defies them. He is convinced he is infinite. The old think young, the indecisive imagine themselves to be the leaders of men, and the ordinary man thinks of himself as an intellectual. Everyone has to do everything every time. No one seems willing to be just a limited something or someone. Hence the despair of possibility. Man fails to appreciate his limitations. He is filled with guilt.

Believing that people are basically innocent, Protestantism tends to see evil outside of the human person. This is directly contrary to Catholicism which acknowledges human weakness and suggests that evil lies within the human person. If the evil is outside of us, then logically we should be able to conquer it and keep it under control.

For the Protestant then, forgiveness and compassion, highly prized virtues among Catholics, are replaced by hard work and individual success—and guilt. Consequently, great moral indignation can be mustered over the failure to conquer this external evil, the suspicion being that people fail, not so much from weakness, but from ill will, from not having tried hard enough. Is it any wonder that in so many Protestant circles, personal sin is denied?

Here then are three concrete values by means of which

you and I can become Catholic Americans rather than American Catholics. Leisure, community, forgiveness. Today our country needs all the resources her people can offer. To look deeply within our Catholic tradition is not a narrow, paralyzing activity. Rather it is a challenge to be concerned about American values. A challenge to discover the best in our religious heritage. A challenge to take our Catholicism and to ameliorate our American culture. A challenge to ask ourselves how we characterize ourselves. Are we American Catholics or Catholic Americans?

TURTLE MORALITY AND AMERICAN MENTALITY

Last August, Watkins Glen, New York, hosted a seven-day rock festival. Like its predecessors, this festival attracted thousands of young adults and teenagers. Entrepreneurs hired several of the finest hard-rock groups in the country to entertain. Miles of tents, sleeping bags, campfires, beer cans, and human beings dotted the terrain. There was a consistent abuse of liquor, drugs, and sex throughout the week. Before the festival ended, three people had died and seventeen more had been hospitalized.

Later, a doctor made a curious comment. "At future festivals," he said, "there should be officially sanctioned drug concessions. Many young merchants at Watkins Glen sold bad drugs. No one really tried to correct this practice. So the best thing to do at future rock festivals is to make clean drugs legally available."

What the doctor is saying seems sensible, practical, and humane. But this very humaneness is at the bottom of a puzzling dilemma, about which I would like to address my remarks this evening. It is the dilemma of what is happening to our American morality, the dilemma by which Twentieth century men and women no longer commit sins, but instead experience life. Consequently, some nasty behavior has suddenly become quite virtuous.

Isn't it very true? No one will deny that doing drugs is today an integral part of America's culture. Yet what is happening is that we are becoming so much at home with the problem, so familiar with people smoking marijuana and popping qualudes, that we are rapidly losing the ability to look at the root elements. The value of not having to rely upon drugs is replaced by the value of helping people cope with drugs. Our concern now is how to help drug-users live comfortably, not to ask why people take drugs in the first place.

Or consider sex. Recently a newspaper quoted the director of a Planned Parenthood chapter telling the Rotary Club that the lack of proper birth control information has added to major problems in the country. At first glance the speaker is right in certain circles. As a matter of fact, it seems odd to even mention birth control anymore. According to *Time* magazine, they stone virgins today. According to television, there is a great deal of nonmarital sex going on. Chastity and monogamy are as outmoded as the horse and buggy. Let's be sensible. Let's be practical. Let's be realistic!

My reply to these statements is simple: "Let's be honest!" We have taken our moral standards and made the exceptions so humane that the original values are fast fading out. We are raising pitifully few strong voices to call a halt to this casualness with which we Americans are slipping into drugs, divorce, abortion, nonmarital sex, and sterilization. And it is that word "casual" that is so critical. We have adopted a morality of casualness. Why? Because we have been propagandized and sloganized into a morality of expediency. There are huge profits in rock festivals, in abortions, and in illicit sex. Technology has made the followup solutions so palatable that any talk of prior restraint, self-control, or discipline is unnecessary.

The after-the-fact concern has become so widespread and so comfortable that we have evolved a turtle morality.

Do you remember the old story of the little boy who found a turtle and made it his pet? One day the turtle suddenly rolled over on its back and died. The boy was heartbroken and would not be consoled. His mother called his father, who rushed home from the office to help the boy in his grief.

Finally the father said, "Look son, here's what we'll do. We'll have a little funeral ceremony, and you can invite your friends (at this the boy stopped crying). Then we'll put the turtle in my silver cigarette box (the boy was interested), and we'll get some ice cream and cookies and have a party afterwards" (the boy was smiling from ear to ear by this time). No sooner had the father said this, than the turtle flipped over on his legs and began to walk away. "Oh daddy," exclaimed the boy, "let's kill it!"

That's turtle morality. The original value is lost in the attraction of the kindly assistance. Everyone is so taken up with the helping hand that they elevate their tragedy into a virtue. The original incident of the turtle's death is no longer important.

Someone has characterized what is happening as the "filter mentality" in our culture. You are familiar with its slogans: "Enjoy the smoke, but not the cancer . . . drink the soda but not the calories . . . have the sex but not the baby."

More eruditely, Dr. Karl Menninger points out that sin is being covered over and camouflaged. We are employing euphemisms, he says, and not calling sin what it is. In his book, *Whatever Became of Sin*, Menninger gives examples. A harried husband murders his nagging wife. Is he sinful? No, he is sick. A fat teenage boy beats up his skinny father. Is he sinful? No, he is misguided. A young woman nuzzles three or four drinks too many. Is she drunk? No, she is high. An unmarried couple do some heavy petting in their flaming red MG. Are they committing sins of impurity? No, they are enjoying release from sexual tensions. Any wonder that the Chinese are puzzled by all this? They have a clever way of describing it. "You Americans are funny people," they say. "You take a drink and pour in lots of liquor to make it hot, then add ice cubes to make it cold. You put in bitters to make it tart, and follow up promptly with sugar to make it sweet. Then holding it up, you say, 'Here's to you!' and drink it yourself!"

A clever illustration of what is happening to our current morality. Sin isn't disappearing, but awareness of it is. Sin isn't changing, but sensitivity to it is. As Menninger so aptly put it, "The modern world has lost its sense of sin."

This is why we must beware of the turtle morality. We live in a country where opinions, measured by Harris and Gallup, can easily become the standard of right and wrong. We live in a country where ethical standards can easily become the same as therapeutic compassion. We live in a country where more energy is being spent on adjusting to the unfortunate wrong situation than on upholding the original moral dictate.

Turtle morality is nothing else but the disease of morally defective nerve endings of the soul instead of the body. It is an indifference to sin. So when we talk about drugs, or divorce, or euthanasia, or nonmarital sex, you and I must not fall into the benign humanitarianism of the doctor at the Watkins Glen Rock Festival. As Christians, we must take a stand on the ground that separates human compassion from religious conviction.

Taking such a stand is not a return to reactionary conservatism. Instead, it is a reminder to all people from the Gospels of Jesus, a reminder to look carefully at what the creeping expediency of turtle morality is doing to our world.

THE HUMAN JESUS

It takes two themes to answer adequately Christ's question: "Who do you say I am?"

Jesus, you are life, and you are human.

Sören Kierkegaard once said that the real stumbling block to Christianity is the humanity of Jesus. It would be much easier to believe in Jesus if he were just God. But to believe in another man, to see our salvation depending on another man, is a hard pill for our proud egos to accept.

Have you ever noticed, for instance, that when a theologian speaks only of the divinity of Jesus and does not refer to his humanity, there is never much of a stir? But let that same theologian speak only of the humanity of Jesus and not refer to his divinity, and you have a real stir. A heretic! A negator of the divinity of Christ! A denier of the fact that Jesus is God!

True, he is God. But Jesus is also man. The humanity of Jesus is very important because everything significant about Jesus occurs in his humanity. God does not reveal anything to us about his divinity. All revelation occurs because, as the Gospel says, "The Word became flesh." Hence we are not redeemed in the divinity of Christ. We are redeemed precisely in his humanity. This is the whole point of the Gospel message. In fact, the only thing that really distinguishes Christianity from other religions man has known, is the fact that we begin with the affirmation that God is a human being, that the Word is made flesh, that the Son of God is a man like us.

Unconsciously this idea that Jesus is human has crept into our literature and our conversation. Perhaps you have heard stories similar to that of the atheist who one day decided to climb a high mountain. He got up to the top all right, but slipped while coming back down. Plummeting downward, he desperately clasped a thin febrile branch protruding from the side. He looked down and could see no one. He looked up and saw no one. Then he looked down again and loudly cried out, "Is there anyone down there who can help me?" No answer. He looked up and shouted the same question, "Is there anyone up there who can help me?" A voice came from heaven, "I can help you." Overwhelmed, the atheist queried, "Who are you?" "I am God," came the response. "Will you help me?" "Yes," said the Lord, "but first I want to know if you will do whatever I ask." "I will," came the firm reply. "Good," said the Lord. "First, do you believe in me?" "I do," said the atheist. "Second, let go of the branch." At this the atheist looked all the way down. Then he looked up again and cried out, "Is there anyone else up there who can help me?"

Humorous? Perhaps. Symptomatic? Definitely. An unconscious turning away from a demanding divinity to a more understanding humanity is characteristic of most of us. This is precisely why the humanity of Jesus is such a powerful theme. Hence we should not speak of a certain victory in the life of Christ as though everything were pre-arranged and programmed. Why? Because then Jesus lives out only a charade, not a real human existence open to shock, unpredictability, and the possibility of failure. These are all part of human experience. If Jesus is authentically human, then he must have been like us in everything except sin; he knew human frailty, imperfection, and inefficiency.

Inefficiency? If there is anything we Americans have a fetish about it is the exact opposite—efficiency. The hills are alive these days, not with music, but with experts trying to make the world a more efficient place in which to live. Look in the Yellow Pages under management consultants, and you will find a yard or two of them. Search the book shelves, and every publishing season will find another set of books on new and improved methods of management. Go to conventions, and you will find that what is proclaimed as new is also proclaimed as efficient. But stop for a moment and ask yourself whether we humans are really very efficient after all.

Albert Camus, the French existentialist, once remarked that the greatest thing a human being can do is to lead a truly human life. Efficiency experts are constantly overlooking this piece of sage advice.

The world simply does not run efficiently. Politicians have understood this for centuries, and they have kept governments going, not by being efficient, but by dealing with people as they are. Those persons who really understand the basic inefficiency of mankind are called diplomats or statesmen. Politics defined as the art of the possible is precisely that, because it is built on an understanding of the way things are actually accomplished in the real world. But it is hard to teach old dogs new tricks. That is why the rising generation can always accuse the retiring generation of some measure of inefficiency and feel wonderfully self-righteous in doing so. It is a safe accusation to make against any generation, because it is true of all of them.

All this has maximum import for you and me. Jesus Christ lived an intensely human life and invites us to do the same. That is the whole meaning of his incarnation. Our Catholic Church, now eagerly turning to management consultants, financial disclosures, and other moves towards efficiency, should ponder the realities of the inefficiency of the human condition. The Church is, after all, a place where people are meant to feel at home, a place where they can grow to their full personhood in Christ Jesus. Is it?

Jesus did not seem to worry much about efficiency. He would have had himself born in the electronic age if he thought that the most efficient means of conveying the Good News was more important than the substance of that message.

So let's ask for a little of this humanity of Jesus. He can only touch us and change us when we drop the armor of efficiency, when we are able to reveal ourselves with all the rough edges showing, and when we profess that to be Christian is to be imperfect.

A recent episode of Peanuts brings this out in a striking way. One day Lucy decides to become a psychiatrist. So she turns over an orange crate and chalks up a sign: "Psychiatric Help—Five Cents." Who stumbles along but Charlie Brown. "Lucy," he inquires, "what do you do if you don't fit in? What do you do if you don't seem to know what's going on? What do you do if you don't know what to do?" Lucy takes Charlie Brown by the hand to the crest of a high hill that overlooks a beautiful horizon. "Do you see that world out there, Charlie Brown?" she asks. "Yes." "Are you sure this is the world in which you are going to live for the rest of your life?" "Yes." "There is no other, you are sure?" "Yes." "Well, in that case, won't you please live in this world, stop complaining, and give me my nickel."

There is a lot more than five cents worth of advice in that statement. If Jesus is to be Savior to us and not Superstar, then we must realize he is life, and he is human. The more we live that life fully, the more completely we accept our humanity, then the more accurately we can answer that all-important question Jesus addressed to Peter, "And you, who do you say I am?"

MODERN DISBELIEF

In a packed ballroom of the Sir Francis Drake Hotel in San Francisco during a recent theological convention, a young woman asked an eminent lay theologian a startling question. "Doctor," she said, "would you mind telling me why you are still a Catholic?" The learned doctor said, "I am a Catholic because for me the faith answers all my problems. *Lord, where else could we go?*" That afternoon the same young woman put the same question to a priest-theologian. "Father, why are you still a Catholic?" The priest thought for a moment and then said, "I am a Catholic because of the resurrection. If Christ has not risen, our faith is in vain." The girl pondered that response for a moment and said, "Father, that tells me why you are a Christian. I asked why you are a Catholic."

If any of you were at that convention last spring, you probably would have been grateful for not being asked this question publicly. But what about privately? What about the youngster in class who tells you he no longer believes in God? What about the child at home who asks you why you do? Why are you a Catholic?

This basic question gravitates around today's 20th-century crisis of faith, a crisis that underlies the whole subject of religious consciousness. This is the crisis of modern disbelief. But why do I say *modern*? Atheism has been with us for 30 centuries. The psalmist declared 1200 years before Christ, "The fool says in his heart, 'There is no God.' " Plato in his *Republic* recounts the atheism of the sophists. The French encyclopedists were atheists, and so were some English authors of the 19th century. What is so unusual about *modern* disbelief? Brutally put, its E.S.P.: its extent, secularity and pedagogical aspect.

First, the extensiveness of modern disbelief. The village atheist popularized by R. Ingersoll in the 19th century has ceased to be an institution of American life, not only because villages have become scarce, but because the unbeliever is no longer a rare specimen.

Today you must take for granted that the majority of persons of letters and science do not believe in God. One of the tangible results of Vatican II was the establishment of the Secretariat on Atheism. We must be painfully aware of the practical unbelief of the masses. Christianity is *not* on the march around the globe. Indeed many modern authors are characterizing our age as the "Epic of the Christian Disaster." We are not marching forward as Christian soldiers.

The author of a new book entitled *They Call Us Dead Men* gives some intriguing statistics about our world. He asks us to imagine the world as a town of 1000 people. In this town would be 60 Americans and the rest of the world would number 940 people. The author says a great deal about how much income we 60 Americans make, and how much we produce, and how much we eat. But his statistics about religion are equally startling. Of these 1000 people in the village of the world, 330 would be Christians (230 would be Catholics, and another 100 would be Protestants) and 670 would never have heard of a rabbi called Jesus. 670—two-thirds of the world! Shocking, perhaps. Symptomatic, definitely.

But how can I personalize my faith? How can I change my God-image from IT to I? One good method is to throw away the word *God*, and substitute the concept, *Father*. Whenever Christ spoke, he spoke not of "God" but of "Father." The only prayer he gave to us was the "Our Father." His last words were, "Father, into your hands I commend my spirit." Today atop Mt. Olivet is a chapel where the "Our Father" is written in 36 languages on stone. Now whether the "Our Father" was spoken on Mt. Olivet or not is unimportant, but the symbolism of having the "Our Father" written in all these languages is important. It is symbolic of the fact that the "Our Father" transcends languages and nations. So too does our personal faith in the Father. So if God is dead, I submit that the term, *God*, is dead. The concept of *Father* is still very much alive.

The second reason for modern disbelief is a philosophy called secular humanism, a philosophy that finds the notion of God irrelevant to what is going on in today's world. This is the age of Biafra, Resurrection City, and Vietnam. Forget that praying stuff, and let's go where the action is.

Imagine for a moment that next Sunday you pick up a copy of the *New York Times* and see the headline, "GOD IS DEAD. Eminent Deity succumbs. Successor in doubt. Nixon orders flag at half-staff."

Under the byline would be this account:

> God, the creator of the universe, deity of the world's Jews, and ultimate reality of Christians, died late yesterday during major surgery taken to correct a massive diminishing influence. His age was not known, but close friends estimate that it greatly exceeded existent beings. In an interview with God's doctor this morning, he noted that God's death was not unexpected, for he had been ailing for some time. He also noted that the death of God had been prematurely announced in 1870 by the famed German philosopher, Nietzsche, but since Nietzsche was insane for the last 10 years of his life, he might have been confused. The doctor said that God had been a good patient, compliant, alert, and cheerful. He did not suffer; he just, as it were, slipped out of our grasp.

He just slipped out of our grasp—that's what the secular humanists tell us. So treat him as we do an ex-president, once a powerful figure, but one who doesn't count for much now. Don't deny God outright, simply ignore his presence. Go to Church on Sunday, but forget about God for the rest of the week. A poet puts it this way:

"Mr. Business went to church, he never missed a Sunday,
And Mr. Business went to hell for what he did on Monday."

As parents and as educators you must show people that God can be found not only under the steeple, but is also manifested among the people. To show that God is relevant you must be a responder, not a reactor. In other words, you must respond positively to particular life situations where the modern nonbeliever would simply react. You who live in faith and hope must not crawl into the womb of invulnerability when disaster strikes and doubts start.

You see, to be a man or woman of faith means to be a responder, not a reactor. It means to take your belief and apply it to the nitty-gritty of life. This is difficult. But every situation evokes both a response and a reaction. Insofar as you and I try to respond more and react less, then we are manifesting our belief in God. Then we are showing our faith in a world of secular humanism.

And so I would like you to think about both of the problems which we analyzed regarding faith. Can the extensiveness of unbelief and the secular humanism that finds God irrelevant to that world, survive when faced with those other two factors: the fatherhood of God and the fact that we are going to respond and not react? I don't think so. Do you? How about answering that girl's question at the Newman Conventions?

THE CHURCH AS A SIGN

Cicely Tyson received an Academy Award for her role in the movie *Sounder*, for her portrayal of a black mother who holds her family together when everything seems to be going against her. *Sounder* is but one of many black films appearing on the market today. It is a thoughtful and charming story of a black family caught in the misery of the Depression. To provide food for them, the father steals meat. He is caught and sentenced to prison. To survive, many things must bind his family together. *Sounder* is the story of this fidelity, a fidelity which can be likened to that of today's Catholic and his Church.

What I am saying is this. The Church affords many deep experiences in your life. It's your first community. It's the six candles flickering around grandmother's casket. It's the kiss of peace of real warmth from someone you never met before. It's standing and talking to people after Mass. It's the conviction that something worth celebrating is afoot in the universe. It's the ballast that keeps you from capsizing when the doctor says, "It's cancer!"

But what has happened to our Church? The so-called traditional notions are breaking up. The Rosary is not the inviolate devotion it used to be. Priests and nuns are leaving their vocations in unprecedented numbers. The relevancy of our Catholic schools, with so many closings across the country, is being questioned. And today people are walking out of basilicas in defiance of Christ's Vicar, the Pope.

Where does that leave us? It leaves us like the family in *Sounder*, with the problem of fidelity. It leaves us with the problem of change. It leaves us with the problem of trying to understand the Second Vatican Council when it said the Church was a sign, a prophet, and a community.

Many modern authors are asserting that the Church is the Pope, the bishops, and us—that everyone belongs to Peter's fragile bark. This is true—true as far as it goes. But it doesn't go far enough. The Church is not just people. It is people and Jesus Christ. The Church is a gathering together of human beings around one human being who is a real man and true God. This is our problem and our glory. The problem is that our part of the Church sometimes looks more like a "multiplication of Archie Bunkers" than of Jesus Christ. The glory is that we are the body of Christ.

Come now, says the hard-headed realist. That's all very romantic and idealistic, but isn't it stretching the point a bit too far? The Church isn't really Christ, is it? It just imitates him, talks about him, right? Wrong! We must come to the crucial question. Is the Church just a group of people following Christ the way that Marxists follow Marx, or weight watchers follow Jean Nidetch, or Indians revere Gandhi, and so forth?

No, the purpose of the Church—as a group and as individuals—is to make Christ visible in the world. Vatican II says, "It is the function of the Church led by the Spirit to make the Father and his Son present and, in a sense, visible—in other words, the Church is a sign!

I'm sure you remember the tragic shooting at Kent State. One of the outcroppings from this tragedy is a poster which depicts a girl kneeling over the body of a slain student. Her arms are outstretched, there is a look of horror on her face. The caption, "Don't forget Kent State."

Interestingly enough, the girl in the picture, the mystery coed, turned out to be not a coed at all, but a fourteen-year-old girl who had run away from her home. Her parents had recognized the picture, and soon she was on her way home to what seemed to be a happy ending to an American tragedy. It turned out to be not an ending but just the beginning. She ran away again, and it's easy to understand why.

When she returned home, she got a reception much like that of the woman in the Gospel who was dragged into the center of the crowd before Jesus and accused of adultery. Other parents refused to have their children see her. The principal of her school suspended her. She was harrassed by the local police and picked up four times for charges which did not hold up in court.

The mail she received was unbelievable—obscene, abusive and vicious. One of the letters contained the pictures of the four slain Kent State students and a picture of her with her face X-ed out with the caption, "It's too bad you weren't shot, too!"

No wonder that girl ran away from home! I wonder if she would have, had Jesus been there to come to her aid, as he did to the accused woman. It's interesting that Mary of Magdala ended up better off than that girl. For the Mary of the Gospel was helped by Jesus and accepted as a person. But this girl wasn't so lucky, and so she ended up the fifth victim of the Kent State tragedy.

One may be permitted to ask why wasn't Jesus there? Why wasn't Jesus there to show her compassion and understanding in her moment of need? Why wasn't Jesus there to tell the crowd "The first one among you who is without sin, let him be the first to send the hate letter, to make the obscene phone call, to try to run her out of town." The real question, of course, is "Why weren't there any Christians there?" Because if the Church is a sign, then it is through men and women who give themselves to the Lord in faith that Jesus desires to extend his love, care, and compassion in the world.

Remember, the Church is not a duty. It is not a privilege. It is the inevitable result of God becoming Man. If he needed to be visible it had to be until the end of time, not just thirty-three years. If God were to speak to man in Hebrew, he would also talk to him in English. So, the Church is His sign.

To whom? And this brings us to the second half of our talk. Having explained the nature of the Church as sign, let us now glance at the object of the Church as sign. Who needs this sign of Christ today? To whom must the Church manifest Jesus? What sign must the Church be in our 20th century?

I think the answer is threefold. Today's Church must be a sign of unity, charity and stability. Unity for those who feel left out. Charity for those who need healing. Stability for those overwhelmed by change.

Today's Church must first of all be a sign of Unity

What do you do if somebody feels like a stranger? You make him feel at home—welcome. Coming out of his prayer, Christ first went to people. By his simple everyday respect for them—all of them—they knew he was offering them a real belonging, a center to go to, a home. The amazing thing about Christ's "new" Kingdom was that it was for everybody. Nobody was excluded: shepherd, Jewish quisling, adulteress, rabbi, child, poor man, leper. He didn't patronize them; he didn't treat them as if they were worthwhile. He treated them as his brothers and sisters because that's what they were.

So what is the Catholic supposed to do after he walks out of 7:30 Mass at St. Mary's after having received Communion? He's supposed to have an overwhelming sense of God's calling all men to that *communion*, to enjoy the riches of home— hippies and hardhats, bigots and beggars, wardens and schol- ars and nursery school toddlers.

The Christian therefore works mightily to counteract the danger that threatens all movements, from Jewish messianism to modern pentecostalism: an aura of elitism, almost unavoid- ably giving the impression to benighted outsiders that "if you don't do what we do, you're not as good as we are"; whereas the real purpose of the Church is to give something away, do something for others. Not to shut people out, but rather to welcome people in.

Today's Church must secondly be a sign of Charity

Read the Gospels and you see the first thing Jesus did was heal. Heal not just "souls" but bodies. As far as I am concerned, this is also the epitaph for a Christian. If you legitimately deserve to have that placed on your tombstone ("And there came a man" or "And there came a woman"), then you will know that you have been a truly human person, open to the spirit of Jesus, concerned about the needs of the world, concerned about healing.

Healing! Interestingly enough, the first miraculous action of Jesus described by the Evangelist St. Mark is the casting out of a devil from a man possessed. Then, to read the New Testament further is to follow a trail of discarded bandages, crutches and stretchers. In fact, Jesus' whole life is a story of healing—from a mother-in-law's fever to Lazarus' unravelling shroud. Do we find a corresponding burst of healing energy in the Church today?

No Christian can be neutral (because Christ is not neutral) about war, poverty or race, the three sores on the American body politic today. He cannot be neutral about violence, either the explosive gun-and-bomb type or the smooth and silent Cadillac violence of entrenched power, deception and "system."

So Catholics, after singing, "They will know we are Christians by our love," had better go out the door and give actual hungry people some actual bread—either straight into their hands or through the hands of legislators, management, labor leaders, editors, teachers, dramatists, columnists, poets, prophets who will push, pull, poke, cajole, threaten, sweet-talk and maybe scare America into being a land of justice and not a nation whose symbol is a gun. It is difficult to be a good Catholic on an empty stomach.

The Church must thirdly be a sign of Stability

What can the Christian say to this world? Instead of wringing his hands because we don't have Latin any more, or because even women can give Communion, he ought to be someone with a gyroscope deep in his innards, like the big ships. That big, heavy wheel keeps the ship straight and vertical in spite of all the winds and waves pounding on the outside. He remains stable. Why? Because of Jesus.

It wasn't all that simple in Christ's day, for that matter. How did you remain faithful to the covenant as well as the 614 laws that religious leaders had compiled? Did you welcome Greeks? How did you get kids to go to temple when they heard all about these "hip" mystery religions? Did you revolt against the Romans or pay their traitorous Jewish hirelings and hope? Why did God let leprosy happen, why exile, why people like Annas and Caiaphas?

What did Christ do for the people bewildered by life? He was self-possessed, Father-possessed. He didn't feel the need to know the answer to every problem the moment it arose. He felt that his Father would provide courage and enough light. He thought that if his Father took care of yellow tulips and red anemones, pigeons and crows, he would provide a man with enough courage and light to make decisions as they were needed—today. He was symbolically telling us of the stability of his Church.

A sign of unity, charity, and stability . . . a sign of fidelity . . . like the family in the movie *Sounder* . . . like today's Catholic and his fidelity as a sign to his Church.

WOMAN AND THE CHURCH

Last Valentine's Day the *New York Times* ran a question-naire in its Sunday Magazine section. Addressed to one half of our country's population, it was captioned: "The Male Chauvinist Test." A series of questions was raised to test the consciousness of the American male, to check on his true feelings about the Women's Liberation Movement. Some of the questions are worth recounting here.

"To help repress some of the sexism built into the English language, would you wince if the pronoun 'she' were sub-stituted randomly for the universal 'he'? For example, a citizen may vote if she is over eighteen!"

"Do you like Jane Fonda as much as you used to—before she started stumping for Women's Liberation?"

At a regional meeting of the National Association of Women Religious last spring, a group of delegates queried: "Why does not the Church immediately approve ordination for any qualified and willing woman?" Why is it that the most blatant example of discrimination in America regarding the treatment of women is the Church?

Regarding this, let us glance at three areas of maximum concern that relate to women and the Church: first, woman created in the image of God; second, married and single wom-en; third, religious and ordained women.

Woman created in the image of God. Aristotle, Aquinas, and Canon Law to the contrary, women today experience themselves neither as incomplete, mutilated men nor as perpetual children. In fact, they are hopeful that the new approach to Biblical exegesis will repudiate statements of earlier scholars who quote the second and third chapters of

Genesis to prove that women are diminished and inferior human beings.

More positively, it seems clear that, in emphasizing woman as taken from man's side and as being bone of his bone and flesh of his flesh, the Biblical author is stressing not the dependence of woman on man but her equality with him, her participation in the same nature and, possibly, the relationship of love that exists between the two.

Finally, the climax of the story confirms this interpretation, inasmuch as the author says: "Therefore, a man leaves his father and his mother and cleaves to his wife, and they become one flesh." Because of this statement, we might even say that the Biblical author is more concerned with the destiny of man and woman than he is with their origin.

Women must ask the Church then to give serious theological study to this idea that women are created in the image of God, that women, as well as men, are complete and equal human beings, and that man is not superior to woman, nor woman to man. Don't let any silverhaired and smiling monsignor try to tell you that the Church has always led the Women's Liberation Movement with her devotion to Mary and her defense of woman's dignity. Remember, there are more ways than one to enslave a woman. You can either shackle her in a dungeon or you can elevate her to a pedestal. Both places don't allow much freedom of movement. In fact, both make fine, dandy prisons.

What is the Church's attitude towards married women today? Despite the theological notion that a husband and wife possess equal rights and dignity, St. Paul's teaching on male headship, on female subordination, and on the head-and-heart relationship is all too commonplace in today's Church. On the one hand the Church seems to define woman biologically—by her motherhood. On the other hand, one of the most neglected apostolates in the Church is the intellectual and spiritual well-being of wife and mother.

Perhaps this is the reason the working mother is becoming such a commonplace phenomenon in the American economy. Did you know, for instance, that in 1950, 9 million out of 18 million working women in the United States were married? In 1960, the ratio was up to 12 million out of 23 million. And today it is 19 million out of 30 million. Of this percentage, fifty percent of the mothers have all their children in school, while twenty-five percent have children under three.

But it is not only the married woman whose needs the Church has failed in some measure to serve. There are the unmarried as well. The teaching of Jesus about the single state is suggested in his statement, "In heaven they neither marry nor are given in marriage." During his life marriage was regarded as a duty for young men and women. Virginity was despised. The Church would do well to emulate this teaching of Jesus Christ. In Catholic countries single women often lack the freedom, the command over goods, and the rights to professional skills that belong to men. Do all Catholics accept fully the statement of the Second Vatican Council: "A mature and single woman is as free and independent a person as a mature and single man"?

Today's Church should encourage flexibility, freedom, and diversity. It should recognize that Religious women, possessing the unity of lived community experience, can offer a unique contribution to other liberation movements. It should, in fact, be open to the role of women in parish team ministries, as extraordinary ministers of the Eucharist.

The noted Protestant theologian, Kristen Stendhal, has declared that the Church must either joyfully accept the emancipation of women or retreat into fantasy, playing at the private game of "First Century Bible Land." Our Church is not meant to be the Church of the hierarchy, the Church of men. It is the Church of Jesus, who when a woman won by his preaching raises her voice and says, "Happy the womb that bore you and the breasts that sucked you," responds with the magna carta of women's liberation, "Still happier are those who hear the word of God and keep it!"

MOTHERHOOD, WOMANHOOD, MARYHOOD

In the Doge's Palace in Venice hangs a fresco covering one entire wall of the spacious Council Hall. The fresco is remarkable for its beauty and preciseness of detail. But one thing that always surprises visitors is that the artist put his wife's face into the painting three times. In each case the woman is quite conspicuous, standing in the foreground in a radiant robe of blue.

In the first scene the wife looks down from heaven with a saintly purity upon her face. Another scene shows her looking up from purgatory with a worried and pained glance. The third scene has her looking up from hell with the horror of unrepentant agony.

These remarkable scenes are a source of constant query for the Palace guides. Each has his own adaptation of the story. But the tale that seems best to answer the meaning of this anomaly was related to me by a Venetian native as we toured his great city during a vacation granted from our theological studies in Rome. The answer, this guide told me, is to be found in the life of the artist. At times his wife was the good angel leading him Godward and heavenward. At times the same wife was his trial, his cross, his purgatory. At still other times his wife was his temptress, an agent of Satan, leading him to hell.

This story may well cause us to lift our eyebrows. Yet it is a true story that poignantly illustrates our first point, the vocation of womanhood. Our present age goes from Adam's Rib to Women's Lib, and it is an age where we see women obviously denying and denigrating their role as women and as mothers to the point of absurdity. It is well to realize that womanhood achieved its true worth only through our Judaic-Christian heritage. The ages have held varying views of woman. The Greeks admired her bodily perfection but said nothing else. The Jews accorded her a secondary role in the Law. The Moslems hid her away as a toy for men. The Christians elevated her as a member of the faith community. But Christianity elevated woman to a pedestal by making Mary the Mother of the Church. The fact of womanhood is just as valid today as it was centuries ago. The fact of the morality of the world depends upon our women.

Yours is also the vocation of Motherhood and Maryhood. If we could today take just one Joyful Mystery of the Rosary, the Visitation, we will see the role of Mary. Many were the Old Testament prototypes of Mary: the fidelity of Ruth, the judgment of Debora, the fortitude of Judith, the heroism of Esther. All this is summed up in the Visitation.

Christian mothers must walk with Mary. This is your privilege and your goal. It must be your resolution to bring Christ to others, as many did over the plains of Esdraelon, the hills of Samaria, and the country of Judah. You must put Christ back into our space age society from which he has been so ruthlessly banished. You must bring him back to the marketplace. St. Paul asks us, "Know you not that you are the temple of God and that the spirit of God dwells within you?" And again, "I live now, not I, but Christ lives in me." And Jesus tells us, "Anyone who loves me will be true to my word, and my Father will love him; we will come to him and make our dwelling place with him."

Like Mary, you must not only bring Christ to others, but, like Elizabeth, you must recognize Christ in others by your example and way of life. Yours is Mary's *fiat*, the *fiat* of acceptance leading to faith, the *fiat* of resignation leading to hope, the *fiat* of compassion leading to charity.

Think back on the Doge's Palace in Venice. Think back on Mary, on yourself, on your vocation. May you always live up to the sublime vocation that is yours, the vocation of womanhood, motherhood, and Maryhood.

GOD IS LOVE

"He who does not love, does not know God. For God is Love."
1 John 4:7-8

During World War II, my dear friends, the great comedian Eddie Cantor spent much time in Paris, visiting the homes for children supported by charity. At these homes, Cantor handed out hundreds and hundreds of chocolate bars to the orphaned younsters.

At one large orphanage, most of the children grabbed the bars eagerly. They clustered around their benefactor joyfully. But, out of the corner of his eye, Eddie noticed one small girl sitting all by herself in the corner. She had a wan face and blond curls. She had not touched her candy.

As soon as he could drag himself away from the throng of admirers, Cantor walked over to the little girl. Kneeling down beside her, he asked: "Now just what can I do for you, young lady?" And then, Eddie Cantor tells us, he heard the two saddest words he has ever heard in all his life. The little orphan looked up at him and said: "Love me!"

"Love me!" This evening, my dear friends, someone else is plaintively pleading for love. She is not at Paris, France—but here at Malvern, U.S.A. She is not a French orphan, but a Jewish mother. And her plea is not for love of the body, but rather for love of the spirit. I am speaking, of course, of Our Blessed Mother. For today's feast—Mary's Assumption—can best be characterized as a Feast of Love.

Within the last fifteen months, much has been written about devotion to Mary. Not a little controversy has been engendered. Newspapers all over the world have been headlining alarming articles: "Is the Council downgrading the Mother of God?" "Is the Catholic Church reversing its Marian Traditions?" "Is the Pope encouraging a Devotional Diminution towards the Maid of Nazareth?"

The answer, of course, is decidedly negative. Such statements do not mirror the mind of our present-day Church. They are simply exaggerations of our Jet-Age Secular Press. Devotion to Mary has always been subservient to devotion to Jesus. The Assumption, for instance, depends upon the Ascension. Today's feast is only a "taking up." The Ascension however, is a "going up." The Creator always precedes the Creature. But—can we honor the Son, and forget the Mother? Can we adore Jesus, without loving Mary?

Life has been compared to a house, a house which boasts three floors. On each floor live people who love. On the first floor of life's house, for instance, dwell people who love things. These are the materialists. Color them green. Their goal— wealth, riches, monetary possessions. Their ambition in life— to look good. On the second floor, however, lives a different class—the men and women who love persons. These are the sensualists. Color them red. Their goal in life—pleasure, passion, sex. Their ambition in life—to feel good. On the third floor of life's house dwells still another group, the human beings who love God. These are the saints. Color them white. Their goal—happiness, holiness, heaven. Their ambition in life—to be good.

Mary is the express elevator to the third floor of life's house, my dear friends. She is the key to how you and I can be good. She is the door to answer Christ's plea—Love me!

You fathers and husbands out there this evening, you are the head of your family—the breadwinner, the voice of authority in your home. Is the love of Mary the keynote of your family life in Christ? How often do your wife and children see you on your knees reciting her Rosary? How effectively are you bringing Mary into your business, your politics, your recreational activities? Men, the world today needs Mary. It is swamped with graft, marital discord, filthy speech. Look about you. Payola, race riots, war abounds on all sides. Our world is desperately concerned with looking good. Any wonder that you and I can be characterized as living in a godless society?

A society which rejects the one thing worth living for, and calls it "Progress."

A society which condones and encourages the earning of a "fast buck."

A society which regards our neighbor solely as a number, a statistic, an IBM card.

A society which devaluates the human person even faster than the dollar bill.

A society which murders unborn infants and calls it "The Liberation of Women."

A society which would put old people out of their suffering and call it "The Betterment of Race."

This is the society in which we find ourselves today. A world living on the first floor of life's house. Won't you bring Mary into that world? As guardians of your home, as leaders of our modern society, won't you teach the world how to love?

You mothers and wives out there this evening, you are the heartbeat of your home. You personify love in your family. Are you so filled up with Mary that her love spills over onto your husband and children? Think back, for a minute, my dear mothers. Back to the greatest moment of your life. The moment that you first held that bundle of human joy in your maternal arms. How gloriously happy you were that day! How generously you promised Mary you would keep your child close to her Child. Have you been faithful to that promise? You know, mothers, your children knew you before they knew God. In fact, to your children you were God. Don't let them down. Keep Mary close to your family. Inculcate into your sons and daughters her heavenly virtues of obedience, purity, loyalty. You who in a sense can be said to create love, teach your family the only important type of love. Lift them up beyond the second floor of life's house. Bring them to Mary.

And you young people out there this evening, you youngsters in the Pepsi Generation. You teenagers with your patron saint, Alexander Graham Bell, what is your attitude towards the Mother of God? Oh, I know that in this wise-cracking, shallow-thinking world in which we live, you often ask yourself: "Does it really pay to be good?" Look about you. Petting is becoming something petty. Obedience is being called as old-fashioned as staying at home on a Saturday night. Cheating is so commonplace—if you don't do it, you're a square. A little gizmo that won't fit into a round hole.

But did you ever think that maybe Jesus sent Mary to help you be a square? To help you stand out from the crowd. To help you obey the Pre-Beatle Commandments. After all, Christ might be reverently termed a Square. So much of a square in fact, he was crucified on a tall cross. And it was this same cross that the bishop traced on your forehead at Confirmation. Why? That you may listen to Mary and be like Christ. That you may take the many exciting years ahead of you and spend them on the third floor of life's house. By being good.

So be we father, or mother, or youngster, each of us can take something away from today's Feast of the Assumption.

For to teach us, Mary is pleading in those pathetic words of that little orphan: "Love Me!" How does the poet put it?

> "With legs to take me where I'd go.
> With eyes to see the sunset's glow.
> With ears to hear what I would know.
> O God, forgive me when I whine.
> I'm blessed indeed. The world is mine."

THE CHANGING CHURCH

Two weeks ago fascinating statistics came out of a meeting in New York City. The meeting dealt with an explosion more shaking than a nuclear bomb—the knowledge explosion. There has been an incomprehensible multiplication of human knowledge. One hundred years ago all human knowledge doubled every 50 years. Today the sum of human knowledge doubles every 10 years.

This brings with it change, bewilderment, and uncertainty. The average Catholic is no exception, living as he does in the tumultuous post-Vatican II era. He or she is trembling like a tuning fork over a multitude of new ideas and unexpected events.

Every time a Catholic turns on the TV or picks up a paper he or she reads of priests and nuns in rebellion. This makes good press, because people go for sensationalism. Of course little is said of the 56,000 American priests who quietly do their work without the stage and the limelight.

But we are living, like it or not, in changing times and a changing Church. Charles Kettering, the president of General Motors, says that "the world hates change and yet change is the only thing that brings progress." But is this true from a religious point of view? Are you and I better Catholics because of what has happened in our Church over the past five or six years?

Instead of deploring what has occurred, let's examine why it has happened.

The *why* behind today's changing Church can be summed up in one word: involvement. Last year, in Herkimer, New York, a terrible accident occurred. A station wagon went out of control and plunged down a steep embankment. The thirty-two year old mother painfully dragged herself from the wreckage, together with four of her five children. But the fifth child and her husband were pinned down. It would be only a matter of seconds before the car would burst into flames. The mother frantically crawled up the slope to the highway for assistance.

A car had already stopped and its driver was observing the wreckage below. "Help me!" pleaded the frantic wife. "Oh, please help me! My husband and child are still in the station wagon." "I'm sorry, lady," the driver replied. "I'd like to help, but I don't want to get involved." With that he sped away.

Terrible as this story is, my friends, it is only one of many transpiring in our modern world. People in New York City are scared of riding that city's subways at night, because if attacked, other riders will simply look the other way. Women like Kitty Genovese of Kew Gardens are being raped, murdered, and butchered within earshot of disinterested neighbors. And every day newspapers speak of the apathetic attitude of Americans in general. A public lethargy is settling over America. There is a stampede on to duck responsibility, a swell against "getting involved."

Unfortunately, this apathy is also permeating the practice of our religion. "Religion makes front page news," says a prominent clergyman, "but its practice is found on the obituary page!" Norman Vincent Peale recently remarked, "Never has American Protestantism had a higher attendance—or a lower influence." And the president of a non-Catholic university, speaking at a Catholic college commencement, put it this way: "The trouble with Catholic education today is this: it is not Catholic enough!" I would like to go a step further. I would say, "The trouble with Catholics today is this: they are not Catholic enough!"

Friends, the word "catholic" means "universal." To be a

Catholic deserving of the name means to be universal in one's outlook, one's point of view. Our religion is not a spectator religion. It does not say, "Look out!" It rather says, "Go all out!" For the role of the Catholic must be an active one. Cardinal Newman once said, "Life is too short for a religion of indifference."

To combat passive indifference and to galvanize Christian awareness, the modern Church is undergoing change. Years ago, the three R's meant reading, 'riting, and 'rithmetic. Today they mean renewal, reform, and reevaluation. Cardinal Newman also said, "To live is to change, and to be perfect is to have changed often!"

Yet, apparently, many Catholics do not give credence to such a statement. They actively resist change. They vehemently oppose the updating of the Church. In fact they closely resemble the three women who went to see a psychiatrist in Chicago. Each went with her child. The first returned to the waiting room flustered. "My, but that doctor is good. He hit the nail right on the head. He told me my big problem is money. I am overly enamored of money. And that's why I called my daughter Penny!" With this the second woman went into the office. She too returned all excited. "Can you imagine it? The psychiatrist said that my problem is sweets. I am too attracted to chocolates, bonbons, and confectioneries. That's why I called my daughter Candy!" At this the third mother stood up. "Let's not bother going in," she said to her son. "You and I had better leave, Calvert!"

Many Catholics are like that. They hear so much about protest, unrest, and change, that they won't even bother to go in and check for themselves. These Catholics view the Church as a supernatural insurance company. Heaven is guaranteed as long as you use your envelope on Sunday. It's almost like a game of Monopoly. Proceed to Tennessee Avenue and if you pass Go, collect so many merits. Don't land in jail, so make sure you hit Confession regularly. To reach Park Place and Board-walk, be sure to take your Communion pill, your weekly barbiturate. Shocking? Perhaps. But sadly, friends, it is all too true. There are many Catholics today who attend Sunday Mass with as much spontaneity as Pavlov's dog. They consider Confession as a sacrament providing "seat belt spirituality." Their concept of religion is Salvation-single-file. They think of the Church as a sacramental filling-station, a drive-in that hands out grace.

Now please don't misunderstand. These people are basically good Catholics. They root lustily over the victories of Catholic college football teams. They contribute generously to the annual Catholic Charities collection. They work eagerly in the ham-and-egg booth at the parish carnival. But here's the rub. For these people, Catholicism is something private, not social. It is something designed to fulfill their own personal needs, not their neighbor's. It is something to get them—and not necessarily anybody else—to heaven. "Why should we hear sermons on stuff like housing and segregation?", these Catholics complain. "What we want is a nice, sentimental sermon about the Trinity up there in heaven. Never mind about practical applications to our modern world. We've got enough to worry about concerning how to get saved. The Church has no business getting involved with the problems of this modern age!"

No business getting involved? In this age of Jacqueline Grennan, Charles Davis, and William Dubay? No business getting involved? In this age of sexual obsession, the Silent Holocaust of abortion, and the God-is-dead theology? No business getting involved? In this age which has a passion for speaking out and an aversion for thinking through?

No business getting involved? Victor Hugo once remarked that no army can withstand an idea whose time has arrived. Believe me, friends, that time has arrived. It is the time to realize that our Catholic Church is suffering from structural sclerosis. It is the time to comprehend that for a growing number of Catholics religion is both a chore and a bore. It is the time to understand that unless you and I go out and get involved for Christ, we are missing the whole point about the meaning of our Catholicism in this post-Vatican II era.

Perhaps an obscure poet summarizes my whole thesis best. His work is entitled, "Our Christian Apathy." It goes like this:

> "When Jesus came to Golgotha, they hanged him on a tree.
> They drove great nails through hands and feet. They made a Calvary.
> They crowned Him with a crown of thorns. Real were His wounds and deep.
> For those were crude, cruel days, and human flesh was cheap.
> "When Jesus came to _____, they simply passed Him by.
> They never hurt a hair of Him. They only let Him die.
> For men had grown more tender. They would never cause Him pain.
> So they just passed down the street, and left Him in the rain.
> "Still Jesus cried: 'Father, forgive them. They know not what they do.'
> And still it rained the winter rain and drenched Him through and through.
> But the crowds went home and left the streets without a soul to see.
> So Jesus crouched against the wall and cried for Calvary!"

Our lack of involvement is the cause of Christ's tears. What is your response to today's changing Church?

CHRIST—REX, DUX, LUX

Christus Rex, Christ the King. At a public trial, with the barren Palestinian hillside in the background, Pontius Pilate, the Roman Governor, put to Christ this question: "So, then, you are a king?" Our Lord replied, "It is you who say I am a king. The reason I was born, the reason why I came into the world, is to testify to the truth."

Today, more than 1900 years later, it is easy for us to answer Pilate's question. The solution is more transparent than the waters of Cana. The kingdom that Jesus speaks of is not of this world. It is a spiritual kingdom. The royalty of Christ is his love, the scepter of Christ is his sacrifice, and the throne of Christ is his cross.

Love of the world and its gold, glamour, and glitter is one of the greatest evils of modern times. Today men and women pay homage not to one true King but to a triumvirate of false kings. Today people kneel and adore as their ruler, not Jesus Christ, but the honors, pleasures, and worthless gold and glitter of the Godless society in which we live, a society that would put old people out of their misery under the euphemism of social betterment, a society of mass-produced food and dubiously produced opinions of a sensationalistic press, a society where religion makes front page news but its practice makes the obituary pages.

This society in which we live today is the king these foolish people adore. This is the royalty they prefer. But this society does not manufacture joy and peace. In God alone can we find true happiness. Jesus has told us, "You cannot serve God and mammon." It must be either one or the other, but not both.

You must make a choice. Why not make it The King and You? Christus Rex—Christ the King.

Christus Dux, Christ the Leader. Through the ages people have searched for heroes whom they could admire. But where is such a leader to be found? Where can we discover a leader worthy of true admiration? Nowhere on this earth! The leaders of this world are but leaders for a day. Their fame endures but for an hour, and even as nations honor them, they pass away and are gone.

Where are all the mighty leaders now? Men like Cyrus, Alexander, Caesar, Napoleon, Hitler, Stalin? They were leaders who once kept the world in awe and at whose voices nations stood still. These were the leaders in whose presence the earth trembled. Where are they now?

You know the answer as well as I. They entered that great valley where pride, ambition, and lust for conquest and earthly grandeur are not passports to eternal glory. They are in a region where humility, love, and purity profit more than all the treasures of this earth. Where then shall we seek our true leader? Where is the worthy hero who leads by the force of his personality, his being, and his presence? One man alone is our leader, Jesus Christ.

Yes, Jesus Christ is our way, our truth, and our life. He is our Leader and has given us one simple command that is the sum and substance of his gospel, his life, his work, and his teaching: "Come, follow me."

This simple command of our Leader applies to our vocation in life, the vocation to be a Catholic Christian and a true person, the vocation of following our Leader and leading others to Christ through our good example.

Suppose someone asks, "Are you a Catholic?" Would you say quite simply, "Look at my life. I go to Mass. I keep the commandments. I deny myself. I love my neighbor as myself. I take up my cross daily. I practice what I profess. I believe"? Could you, in all truthfulness, give such an answer? In fact, we all are giving that answer unconsciously day by day through the force of our example. The Catholic Church is judged every day in offices, in factories, in fields, in market places and playgrounds. The good name of the Church is in your keeping.

In these days of movies such as "Jaws" and "Super Sharks," you and I may never be rescued from shark-infested waters by a heroic sea captain, but we do have the chance of being rescued from sin-infested waters by a heroic Leader. He is Jesus Christ, who beckons you to lead other people to him by your good example, the example of Christus Dux, Christ the Leader.

Christus Lux, Christ the Light. Jesus Christ said, "I am the light of the world. He that follows me, walks not in darkness, but shall have the light of life." Christ as the Light of the World is an absorbing figure. "God is light and there is no darkness in him," says St. John. But only by serving this Light is it possible for us to attain this truth and holiness for ourselves.

The natural light of the sun promotes and maintains life in plants, animals, and people. The supernatural light of the Son of God causes the seed of grace to germinate in our hearts. Today this same light is beckoning to us through the darkness. It is inviting us to come into its warmth and brilliance. It is encouraging us to serve Christ the Light of the World.

The problem is that although Christ is the Light of the World, the light seems nearly extinct today in Russia. It is growing dim in China. Do not let this light flicker even in the free world. As Catholics, as those who serve Christ, we must be light-bearers. Let us recall the compelling motto of the Christophers: "It is better to light one candle than curse the darkness." And let our candle be our devotion, our zeal for Jesus

Christ in the Eucharist. With such a relationship to light and life available, why walk in darkness? Won't you bask in the sunshine of the Lord?

We all have priorities, and they tell us more about a person than anything else. There can be no priority more important for us than discipleship in Jesus Christ. This is more crucial than any discovery, invention, event, war, or treaty.

Robert Kennedy once said, "Some people see things as they are and ask why; others see things as they might be and ask why not." Today I ask you, "Why not? Why not be the dedicated follower of Jesus Christ that you are called to be? Why not make the word of God required reading in your life? Why not make Christ a familiar relation in prayer? Why not be a Christian in the full sense of the word? Why not?"

The Son of God came as Christus not to get but to give. He saved us and showed us that the things we covet may not necessarily be the best things in this life. Jesus came for you, so the Lord be with you, and you be with the Lord . . . Christus Rex, Dux, Lux. Christ your King, Christ your Leader, Christ your Light.

MARY: SYMBOL FOR TODAY'S CHRISTIAN

On December 3, 1967, Father Walter Burghardt delivered an address about the Blessed Mother. The place was the National Shrine in Washington, D.C., and the occasion was the dedication of the west apse of the shrine. This apse honors five Jesuit saints and was built with $800,000 in donations from the Society and its benefactors. Father Burghardt was invited because he was both a Jesuit and a leading Marian scholar. To his surprise, however, he first had to face a delegation of Jesuit seminarians who were blocking the entrance to the apse. The seminarians were picketing to protest the expenditure of money on the shrine instead of on the poor.

Father Burghardt's opening remarks were colored by this encounter. "Not all my fellow Jesuits are happy today," he said. "Some feel this shrine should be left unfinished. Like the Cathedral of St. John the Divine in New York City, this edifice should be a prophetic symbol that our society is still as rough-hewn, ragged, broken, and incomplete as the building itself. I disagree. If an unfinished cathedral points a prophetic finger at the present, at man's inhumanity to man, a perfected shrine may well point to the future, at man's hope for man. Let those who are not happy with these mosaics and statues and windows; let those who proclaim that, like Mary's ointment, these items could have been sold and the money given to the poor; let them remember the name of the disciple who first denounced this extravagance. He was called Judas, the disciple Jesus himself rebuked for his blindness."

In our age prayer beads are now more meaningful than rosary beads. Coming to Jesus through Mary seems superfluous, even silly. An immaculate conception, a virginal motherhood, a body-and-soul assumption, turn off some Catholics today. They do not disbelieve, they simply do not care.

Such a viewpoint may be frightening. It is certainly challenging, because such a viewpoint compels the Catholic community to ask itself again, "What is the significance of Our Lady in 20th century life? What is beneath Mary's unique conception, her unparalleled motherhood, her unexampled resurrection? What must a Catholic preserve in his Marian vision, even if he discards lifeless beads and living rosaries, the May devotion and the vigil light, all the practices that were second nature only yesterday? What is the dynamic lesson of Mary for every Christian—man and woman, young and old, cleric and lay, conservative and liberal, living in the year 77, 1977 or 2077?"

The symbolism of Mary is the answer. Not symbolism in the sense of fairy tale or make-believe, but symbolism in the sense given by Karl Rahner, who says symbol is the real essence of something. Symbol is that which gives a thing its meaning. In this sense, I speak of Mary as symbol, model of the Church, proponent of feminism, protector of environment, and guardian of virtue.

The Marian symbol stands, first of all, for model of the Church. We all know that the Mother of Christ does not exist in splendid isolation, raised by her prerogatives above the common herd. Quite the contrary. Mary's meaning for today's Christian lies in the fact that God has first and perfectly realized his design for the whole Church in Mary. You and I are the Church. So, what Mary is, that we are destined to be.

When we are talking about Mary, therefore, we are ultimately saying something about ourselves. We are proclaiming the Christian idea of a human person. To be Christian is to commit ourselves to Christ and to others. Mary is the perfect Christian. Why? Because of her *yes* at the Annunciation. By that yes, Mary realized the mystery of the Church to come. By that yes, God came to her and the world. By that yes, God and humankind became one. This is why Vatican II could call Mary the model of the Church. The task of the believing Church is to continue through space and time Mary's murmured yes. Your vocation and mine is to say yes to Jesus and bring him to birth in our human community.

So the symbol of Mary, model of the Church, pervades each of her prerogatives. The Immaculate Conception reveals our redemption and the Assumption our transformation. Mary's first human moment declares dramatically that love begins above, that oneness with God starts with God. God gives the beginning. Mary's first human moment reveals God's incomparable love for a human person and through this one human person his love for us all. Mary's first human moment is proof that God is faithful to his promise—a promise that the same love which enveloped Mary will be ours. Her God will be our God.

The Marian symbol stands secondly for herald of today's feminism. In a recent apostolic letter, Pope Paul VI described Mary as a "new woman" whose example supports the liberating energies at work in the world. The Pope wrote: "The modern woman, anxious to participate with decision-making power in the affairs of the community . . . will note with pleasant surprise that Mary . . . was far from being a timidly submissive woman. . . ."

Her own song, the *Canticle of Mary*, proves this. Many of us have prayed this song for years without realizing the radical implications of the words. It is not exaggerating to call it a revolutionary song. It begins with Mary, the choicest of God's creatures, identifying herself with the poor as they struggle for liberation and humanization. "He has looked upon his lowly handmaid." We have always had difficulty dealing with that title. Throughout history we have felt more comfortable in speaking of her as a queen and adorning her statues with rich clothes and jewels. But Mary has identified herself with the poor, whom Jesus called blessed.

The really radical point of the song comes when Mary describes God's action in the world. "He has pulled down princes from their thrones and exalted the lowly. The hungry he has filled with good things, the rich he sent away empty." This is a description of God's revolution. The established order is completely upset. The dispossessed become the possessors.

Now I do not mean to link today's state of women with the poor, lowly, and hungry, but many feel women need liberation too. Mary can be a symbol of how a woman ought to be free to develop the energetic, task-oriented dimensions of her personality necessary to complete the revolution. In Mary we have an excellent model for social action, for involvement in building the Christian kingdom of justice and peace, for Christian liberation. From the beginning of time men have been ruling the world. As far as I can see, the world is still collapsing. The Marian symbol says now is the time for the world to turn to woman. Here is the meaning of Mary for today's Christian. She is symbol: model of the Church and herald of feminism.

Robert Heilbroner, a distinguished intellectual, says there is no hope for humankind. In a recent book, he suggests that we replace Mary with Atlas as our religious symbol. Why? He says the Titan who carries the burden of the world on his shoulders is more realistic for our lives. Atlas can inspire us to stoically bear our responsibilities as we await the world's end.

I emphatically disagree. If it comes to a choice between Heilbroner's Atlas and the Christians' Mary, I have no doubt which symbol modern-day Christians will choose. Atlas? Who ever sang a song of love for him? Who ever wrote a poem to him? Who ever built a national shrine in Washington to him?

HAPPINESS

"If a man wishes to come after me, he must deny his
very self, take up his cross, and begin to follow in my
footsteps. . . . What profit would a man show if he
were to gain the whole world and destroy himself in
the process?"

From the Gospel according to Matthew

In 1923 an important business meeting was held in the
Windy City of Chicago. The site was the fashionable Edgewa-
ter Beach Hotel. The topic discussed: making profit. The
persons attending: nine of the world's most successful
financiers. Those present were:

The president of a large steel company
The president of a large utility company
The president of a large gas company
A successful wheat speculator
An official of the New York Stock Exchange
The greatest "bear" of Wall Street
A member of the president's cabinet
The head of the world's largest monopoly
The president of the Bank of International Settlements

The meeting was a resounding success. The group of nine
split up and went their separate ways. To the casual onlooker,
that meeting was historic. A gathering of the world's most
successful men. A pooling of clever financiers, astute businessmen who had found the secret of making huge profits.

Yet, to the same onlooker twenty-five years later, a startling difference appears. By 1948 three of these financiers had
committed suicide. One had gone insane. Three more had

died abroad, insolvent and fugitives from justice. The last two were pardoned from prison for the express purpose of dying at home.

Thus perished all nine men, successful financiers who had learned well the secret of making a profit. But they had failed to learn another secret—that money alone does not bring happiness. This is the secret that the poor seldom believe and the rich never forget.

The Bible points out this paradox of self-denial and happiness. But do we grasp this paradox, we who live in an age of mass produced food and dubiously produced opinions, an age whose gods are the latest fashions, the newest novel, the most recent gossip, and the best pills? The very thought of any type of denial, not to speak of moderation, is looked upon as an antiquated flashback to prehistoric times. We are obsessed with a desire to modify and modernize. And yet one cannot but wonder if, with all our concern for external appearances and adaptation, we are overlooking the internal renewal of our Christian lives. For the answer we need not go any further than the words of Christ in the Gospel: "What profit would a man show if he were to gain the whole world and destroy himself in the process?"

So let us speak today, not of profits but of human happiness. As the prophet Jeremiah says, "You duped me, O Lord, and I let myself be duped. You were too strong for me, and you triumphed."

In these days of space satellites, religious bewilderment, and changing values, it seems that psychology is more and more taking the place of religion and divine grace in many circles. Ours indeed is a restless world. It is the age of enormity and conformity. Yet there is one basic desire in every living thing. This characteristic remains constant despite the miniskirts and the minibrains, despite the wars on poverty, the wars on human rights, and the louder wars, small but real, in pockets around the world. It remains stable despite the sickness and suffering, despite disease and death, despite the anguish and the agony. This basic desire shared by every person is the desire to be happy.

Living as we do today in an age of sophistication, affluence, and materialism, one must often ask oneself whether this is really the beginning of a new era of hope and happiness, or an approach to the end of all those hopes and happiness that forever spring from the human heart.

"Do not conform yourself to this age," says Paul in his letter to the Romans, "but be transformed by the renewal of your mind so that you may judge what is God's will, what is good, pleasing, and perfect." As Christians of the new covenant, we cannot anticipate instant salvation along with our instant coffee, much less an easy religion coupled with easy payments. Self-denial is essential to bring us back to the basics of our existence. No one in their right mind ever claimed that Christianity is supposed to be easy and that it does not require a strong backbone. Does not Christ say in the Gospel, "If a man wishes to come after me, he must deny his very self, take up his cross, and begin to follow in my footsteps"? Today more than ever we need a strong backbone of determination to follow Christ. The successful Christian is he who matches his backbone to his wishbone in his quest for happiness.

But how can we achieve happiness? Andrew Carnegie, the famous philanthropist, said that happiness consists of renunciation. *The Baltimore Catechism*, which we studied years ago, put it so simply: "God made us to know, love, and serve him in this world, and to be happy with him in the next life." St. Augustine says, "Our hearts were made for you, O Lord, and they will never be happy until they rest in you."

Happiness is tricky. It is within the reach of all, but with difficulty we grasp at it and with equal difficulty we hold onto it. It is a precious possession. It is a pearl of great price. If we are to be happy, if we are to have lasting peace, if we are to be content in mind and soul, we must perform the difficult. We must do what most Americans absolutely refuse to do. We must surrender unconditionally to the will of God.

God made us for happiness, and every human has that God-given drive to seek happiness. The trouble lies in the fact that millions of human beings confuse happiness with pleasure, and when they stop at pleasure, they are puzzled and perplexed by the emptiness of their hearts and the shallowness of their lives. Happiness will give us pleasure but pleasure alone will never give us lasting happiness. St. Paul told the Romans, "If you live a life of nature, you are marked for death. If you mortify the ways of nature, you will have a life of happiness."

Last year the *London Tablet* asked this question: "Who are the happiest people on earth?" These were the four prize-winning answers:

1. A craftsman or artist whistling over a job well done.
2. A little child building sand castles.
3. A mother, after a busy day, bathing her baby.
4. A doctor who has finished a dangerous operation and saved a human life.

No millionaires among these, one notices. No kings, no emperors. Riches and rank, no matter how the world strives for them, do not make happy lives.

May I add a fifth answer to that list: a happy person is a Christian who has found God, who realizes that the Catholic life is an epic not of Paradise Lost but of Paradise Regained. Despite our many faults, foibles, and failings, we constantly struggle to get up and to continue our steps so that some day we will receive the reward promised us in the first beatitude of Our Lord: "Happy are the poor in spirit, for they shall possess the kingdom of heaven."

Today this is another historic meeting, a meeting which

can terminate in only two outcomes. Will you imitate the nine financiers of that 1923 Chicago meeting, or will you face yourself, face your God, and face your Christian calling?

As the Gospel says, "What can a man offer in exchange for his very self? The Son of Man will come with his Father's glory accompanied by his angels. When he does, he will repay each man according to his conduct."

GETTING POOR

"Christ impoverished himself for your sake, when he was so rich, so that you might become rich through his poverty..."

An old story in the book *Gesta Romanorum*, dating from the Middle Ages, tells of a prince famous for his fleetness as a runner. No one in the kingdom could match his speed. One day a wily old man challenged the prince and won the race. To accomplish this feat, he stuffed his cloak with all sorts of trinkets, gold pieces, and baubles before the race. Then in the course of the race, he tossed them a few at a time along the roadside. Attracted by their shining colors, the prince would stop to admire them each time. As a result, the old man crossed the finish line while the young prince was still admiring the trinkets.

In the spiritual race we all run, the world tosses out many gold pieces, baubles, and trinkets to catch our attention and to divert us from the race. But poverty puts beyond our sight and reach the things of this world that may make us forget our pledged goal of going surely and swiftly to Christ.

In modern America we live on a crest of affluence, a wave of materialism, and the gold and the glitter of the good life. Most of us do not know what real poverty is. We have it too good. We scramble for the almighty dollar and then immediately flaunt and debase the money we make. Detachment from everything is a concept that dates back to prehistorical times. The paradox of history is the fact that money brings little real happiness. This is a fact that people of poverty seldom can believe and that the people of means seldom can forget.

The Christian must embrace poverty. By reason of our

baptism we took a quasi-vow of economy. To come close to Christ we must at times have less than what is necessary, as he did. Remember those provocative words of his Sermon on the Mount: "Blessed are the poor in spirit, for they shall possess the kingdom of heaven." The corollary is just as true. Unhappy are the rich in spirit for theirs will be a frustrated, miserable existence. It's the old story: our wants are always much more than our needs.

Yes, Jesus Christ lived with and loved the poor of his day. "The foxes have their holes and the birds of the air their nests, but the Son of Man has nowhere to rest his head." What is going to happen when the Lord and Judge of all history asks us to render an account for our stewardship during a life of cool, casual, and comfortable living? His Christian message was spread the hard way, not by the law of Wall Street, but by the law of the Good News.

In America today, if one does not have a large wedding, a large funeral, a large house, or a large car, he is regarded as a small pauper. The only thing that is reluctantly tolerated is a large mouth. It takes a person three years to learn how to speak properly and seventy years to learn how to keep his or her mouth shut. But poverty is not a disgrace; it is a plus sign. Pericles said this to the Greeks 500 years before Christ. History tells us that nothing great was ever achieved without much pain. Job tells us that "iron must be tried by fire." And Christ tells us that "he who does not take up my cross is not worthy of me."

The spirit of Christ is that of a pilgrim, someone on his way. The pilgrim has to travel light and poor. Otherwise if a person acquires too many possessions, he or she will be unable to travel at all. The Christian life is a pilgrimage, not a pleasure trip. We witness God by our life and our will, not by the strength of our bank book.

Money doesn't always bring happiness. A man with ten

million dollars is no happier than a man with nine million. Many Americans live off borrowed money. In the richest nation in the world, there are twenty-five million poor, and we should realize that two-thirds of the world have less than $8.00 a month per person. Realize that our country's vast stockpile of surplus food costs 365 million dollars merely to store. Yes, poverty is a perennial problem and a paradox.

Our materialistic culture is painfully subjected to the whims of capitalism. Nowhere, except perhaps in the analogous society of pagan Rome, with its breakdown of family and its craze for pleasure, has every evil been fostered for the sake of making money.

Man becomes like unto that which he loves. If he loves gold, he becomes like gold, cold and hard. The more he gets the more he wants and the more he believes he needs. The sense of the spiritual becomes deadened, and God becomes less and less a reality. Without the spiritual, man becomes a hybrid whose productive results for God and country are self-defeating.

We close with the splendid words of the poet who said:

> "Money will buy clothes,
>   but not character.
> Money will buy a house,
>   but not a home.
> Money will buy medicine,
>   but not health and life.
> Money will buy company,
>   but not love and friendship.
> Money will buy cosmetics,
>   but not beauty.
> Money will buy recreation,
>   but not joy and happiness.
> Money will buy a prominent place in the world,
>   but it won't buy an entrance into heaven."

THE CHURCH AND THE SACRED

A new era in American theater began on the evening of April 29, 1968. On that date, a select audience in New York, at the Baltimore Theater, witnessed the gala premier of *Hair*. For the first time, the curtain went up on this controversial Broadway show. For the first time, the orchestra broke into "This is the Age of Aquarius." Since then *Hair* has signaled a revolution on Broadway. A revolution which has become a part of your life and mine.

Revolution. The word is proclaimed with bravado, or whispered in fear. Revolution, a meaning that is violently debated. To some revolution is necessarily urgent, reckless, and bloody. Its principles are to be found in the thoughts of Chairman Mao. Its heroes are to be found in the Che Guevara's and Ho Chi Minh's.

To others, revolution is hot, then cold, then hot again depending on the circumstances. A demand for reparations. A confrontation, an assault, a march. To history, that tired old but much experienced man who smokes his pipe and slowly scratches his head, revolution is merely a more active part of a passing parade already destined to become less significant, less exciting, less remembered than the events to come.

To you and me, any one of us who has lived through these post-Vatican II years, revolution is very much alive, and we too even unconsciously join Bob Dylan in singing, "The times, they are changing, they are a-changing." Whether this change is good or bad, whether it be violent or non-violent, the fact is that revolution is now. And one thing that you all can be sure of, is that it is the direction of our Church that is at the forefront in this revolutionary age of Aquarius. This direction has taken on two major trends. A trend toward the sacred and a trend toward the social.

Today, we mention the trend toward the sacred. Edward B. Fiske, the religious news editor of the *New York Times*, recently made an interesting statement. He said, "In the past two decades, while churches have been becoming more worldly, the world has been, believe it or not, becoming more religious. While churchmen have been more concerned with making Christianity more secular, society has been looking for the sacred."

Such a statement, in our age where religion makes the front page but its practice makes the obituary page, seems mighty incredible. But today, our revolution is a witness. Witness the increased interest in the occult, in witchcraft, and in eastern religions. Witness the resurgence of meditation, of chanting, of mind expanding drugs. Witness the rapid popularity of *Jesus Christ Superstar*. "Grab a hold of the hand of the Man from Galilee" and "I want to touch you Lord." The statement becomes more credible.

What is happening is this. God is alive today, but science is dead. In our era, the God is dead theologians were monopolizing the publicity. But then a change took place. Thomas Meehan writing in *Horizon* magazine, submits that during the past 50 years, we Americans have seen one technological advancement after another. From the pop-up toaster to the ability to land men on the moon. However, in the past five years, a significant number of Americans have entered upon a headlong flight from reason. A mass retreat into irrationality, anti-rationality and para-rationality. They are sick and tired of playing hide and seek with Almighty God.

Why the change? Why this turn to the sacred? I think you all know the answer. Reason is at best, a monarch. Once it tries to become a tyrant, once it tries to squelch man's need to contemplate, once it tries to squash man's need to dream that impossible dream, man intuitively revolts against it. That is why we have the two main responses in the Church of today. The response of our liturgy and the response of our mysticism.

Take the response of our liturgy. It is really fascinating. At a time when priests are taking off vestments, the hippies are putting them on. At a time when some have been naive enough to stop saying the rosary, the flower children are buying love beads and prayer beads. At a time when some bishops are throwing away their pectoral crosses, a whole generation of Americans are wearing peace symbols around their necks. At a time when we are dangerously close to ridding ourselves of a tradition of 2,000 years in the Church's liturgy, many people are celebrating liturgies filled with incense, poetry, solemnity and awe. No wonder the Almighty must laugh at us and Old Man History must scratch his head.

Overdrawn? Perhaps. Symptomatic? Definitely. For so many of us, the ritual is supplanted by the rational. For so many of us the liturgy is a chore and a bore. For so many of us the Mass is an event to be taught, not an experience to be caught.

Secondly, how about our response to mysticism? You and I haven't seen any Catholic mystics lately. There are all kinds of revolutionary people in San Francisco, Chicago's north side, and New York who are contemplating for hours each day. I was fortunate to have spent some time in Japan two years ago, examining Zen Buddhism. The chief religion of Japan is Shintoism. Curiously this religion boasts no statues, images, or pictures. In fact, its main shrine near Kyoto houses as its most sacred object a mirror. The whole thrust of these Oriental religions is self-perfection.

This is why mysticism can be such a dynamic response to the world. If you and I, the original Jesus People, do not meditate or reflect, it would seem that we have ignored one of the deepest hungers of modern man. It would seem that we

have ignored one of the finest traditions of our Catholic Faith.
Our mysticism.

In the words of the poet: Take care to wonder at the
world. Never hurry by an open door. You live in a universe of
miracles galore. Look for God in small things, the rain, the
sand. Praise Him whenever you find Him in anything small.

If we do this, we uphold our traditions of the liturgy and
mysticism. Let modern man see in us Catholics the place of the
sacred. Let modern man see in us people committed to God.
Let modern man see in us Catholics, what he is searching for.
And then the sad cry of Gandhi will be forever silent: "If only
you Christians were more like Christ."

THE CHURCH AND THE SOCIAL

One of the most important trends of today's contemporary society and today's contemporary Church is the trend towards the social, the trend towards what is called "Community."

Recently an atheist fell off a cliff. On his way downward, he frantically reached up and caught hold of a branch. He looked all the way down and shouted, "Is there anyone down there?" No answer. So he looked all the way up and shouted, "Is there anyone up there?" With this, a voice answered, "Yes, I am here!" "Who are you?" frantically asked my friend. "I am God and I can help you." "Then save me," begged my friend. "First, do you believe in Me?" "I do," was the response. "Will you do anything that I ask you?" "I will," my friend yelled. "Good," said the Lord. "Let go of the branch." At this my friend looked all the way down, then all the way around. "Is there anyone else around here who can help me?" he pleaded!

The factualness of this story can be questioned; but the fact that today's men and women are desperately looking for someone to help them live better lives cannot. In fact if contemporary trends can be believed, the trend towards community is paramount among today's population.

Just take a look around the country. One major urban archdiocese has over 200 underground parishes, each usually led by a priest who, while he continues his traditional ministry, is fairly disillusioned with its effectiveness and relevance. We have communities arising from the Cursillo experience, from Pentecostalism, from Jesus Freaks, from sensitivity sessions, and from group psychology, in which the standard lines are that "We are alone and frustrated and are able to find meaning only by being open, uninhibited, and real . . ." Of course, Jesus Christ said the same thing but he didn't have all the academic confetti and the ten dollar words of today, so he is considered outdated.

An exaggeration? I don't think so. The basic question is why the rush towards the intimate, the intense, the interpersonal. Where does the Church stand? The Blessed Trinity was the first symbolic Christian commune—Father, Son, and Holy Spirit. The early Christians certainly were commune-minded. They had to be. They were often threatened by persecution and could look to no one but themselves.

Can the Church answer this need for community in today's world? Ladislas Orsy gives an answer. This famed theologian has said, "If your Church is sick—make it well. If you can't make it well—you must be part of the problem." But how do we reconcile this?

The "sixties" was a decade of division: conservatives vs. liberals; doves vs. hawks; blacks vs. whites; students vs. administration; priest vs. hierarchy; violent vs. non-violent.

Old words took on a new meaning. Marches were no longer parades. Demonstrations were no longer free advertising. Panthers were no longer synonymous with African wildlife.

Now in the "seventies"—hair has become longer, skirts and pants shorter, life styles poles apart in the same neighborhood. The one word which should describe the greatest depth of essence and meaning of all—LOVE—has been drained and exploited.

Isn't it true? You have a role as a Church Reconciler in a city where the streets are far from being safe; in a country grieved about taking a quarter of a million lives abroad yet increasingly bold about aborting many times that number here at home.

We live in a world full of demilitarized zones; not only between North and South Vietnam, but between Black and White Americans, between Israelis and Arabs, East and West Pakistanis, between Irish Protestants and Irish Catholics. We realize with sorrow that wherever there are preached lies, there too is air pollution. Where suspicion and distrust is spread, there too is germ warfare. Wherever the young are taught to hate, there again is defoliation.

As Catholic Reconcilers, we have a mission to reconcile people to the Church—the greatest commune in the community. This demands fidelity—this demands loyalty. Why? Because it is fashionable to knock our Church. Because a new religion of naturalism seems to be springing into being. Because this new religion will accept no authority except oneself. Because it separates the living flesh of the Mystical Body from the dry bones of the Ecclesiastical Structure.

Facetious, perhaps—symptomatic, definitely. What these people woefully overlook is this: the Church is divine as well as human. Trying to separate the invisible Christ from the visible Church is like trying to divide the seamless robe. It is impossible to have faith in God and not in His Church.

It is our duty to demonstrate our faith in the Church as the greatest living commune of believing men and women in the world. For if we abandon it, who will renew it? I think a popular movie best sums up this idea. *Time* magazine loved it. The *Washington Post* panned it. Critics said it was all the things movies weren't supposed to be anymore but it broke attendance records for days in movie houses across the country. I am speaking of course of the film, *Love Story*.

Love Story, starring Ali McGraw and Ryan O'Neal, heralds a new kind of romanticism that characterizes life in the United States. It preaches a masterful sermon about today's Church and our place in it. Recall, for instance, the scene in which Barrett notices a medal around Jenny's neck. He asks, "Why did you leave it?" "Leave what?" replies Jenny. "The Church" is the response. "Oh, the Church," says Jenny. "I didn't leave it—I never really joined it."

"I never really joined it." How many people in today's revolutionary society are like Jenny? Uncommitted—Catholics in name only. As Frank Sheed says, "Pagan minds with Catholic patches, desperately searching for answers to the sacred, to the community."

It is to these people that you and I are called. Will we respond? My dear people, we must discover the world—the revolutionary world of the Age of Aquarius.

BEING HUMAN

One of New York City's most celebrated sights is Rockefeller Center. Located between Fifth Avenue and the Avenue of the Americas, this prominent site occupies over twelve acres and includes more than fifteen buildings. Here stand, for instance, the famed Radio City Music Hall, the spacious television studios of the National Broadcasting Company, and even an elegant, artificial lake. Rockefeller Center is famous also for its glittering bronze statue of the Greek titan Atlas.

Standing before the facade of a huge building in the Center, Atlas carries the world on his mighty shoulders. He bends forward, as if straining under the tremendous weight. The pressure of bearing the world is skillfully manifested in the statue. Atlas's muscles bulge; his veins stand out. The severe strain of carrying the world becomes the dominant impression for the many sightseers.

Directly across the street from this straining Atlas is a startling paradox. Facing the statue is St. Patrick's Cathedral. Inside the center door of this Catholic church is another statue of another person supporting the world. The figure is the Christ Child. Gracefully seated near the center aisle, Jesus is serenely holding the globe of the world in the palm of his hand.

A fascinating paradox. On one side of Fifth Avenue is Atlas, struggling mightily in his attempt to carry the world on his shoulders. On the other side of the avenue is Christ, serenely holding the world in the palm of his hand. Atlas and Christ. What striking images for our era! It seems to me we are living today in an age that has found the atom, but lost God.

Why are we misguided? As life passes us by, year after year, why don't we become better? The answer is simple: we're human. As long as you and I are human, we're going to have a difficult time loving God. As long as we're human, it will always be easier to slip back than to climb ahead.

Periodically you and I need a new supply of chalk—to analyze our progress in finding God. We need to recall that there is only one difference between a sinner and a saint. A sinner has a past, but a saint has a future. And you have a future that can be realized.

Living as Christians in this century, you face challenges that surpass those of the Greek titan Atlas trying to carry the world on his shoulders. How you meet the challenges that face you will mark you as either brave or cowardly, loyal or traitorous, similar to those who are with Christ, or similar to those who abandon Christ. As St. Paul so pointedly says, "Conduct yourselves in a way worthy of the gospel of Christ."

This is the challenge of your life, of your creed, of your spiritual survival; namely, to care, to share, and to dare.

How well you can respond to this challenge on a day-to-day basis will determine your survival, sanctity, and sanity in today's world where, in many quarters, to be in, you have to be far out.

Your first challenge is to care. For most of us, success is often a progression of failures, but the success of our Christian vocation is usually the result of learning to care. Once you have a caring spirit, you find that nothing is impossible for those who are willing. Christ wants us to love not with words only but with works.

Your second challenge is to share. This means being open and stressing the fundamentals of the faith. Christians can never court isolationism. We are of the marketplace whether we like it or not. In our world of vanishing absolutes, it takes day-to-day courage and concentration to persevere. That is why Christ said, "He who perseveres till the end will be saved." Sharing is not a weakness, but a discipline. It takes courage to share. It takes courage not to compromise our principles. It takes courage to act more and talk less. But as St. Paul tells us, "You are not your own," you who share the faith of Christ. And love isn't love until you give it away.

Your third challenge is to dare. We bravely step into the darkness because we believe in what we profess and we dare to follow his challenge. Christianity will never prevail until Christians dare to put it into practice. For us, it is the will, not the power, that is lacking. Perhaps we who live in the well-organized parts of Christ's mystical body are deceiving ourselves. The uncomfortable Christ might be just too much for us to bear.

We ask you to do some deep soul-searching. We ask you to talk to your God. We ask you, what better time is there to analyze your problems? What better time to seek an answer to the challenge of caring, sharing, and daring?

Christianity is a reckless gamble on a better world to come, but we have an exit. Christianity, of all the beliefs known to man, is the boldest, for it affirms a hope in an after-life which this world vehemently represses. That is why we see a new dimension and a new destiny for humanity.

Your humanness will always make your beliefs difficult to live by. Pain and trouble will always be knocking at your door. There are too many high voltage Catholics today who want only the wine and the roses, and not the reality which this life poses. Belief does not protect you from trouble, but it does help you to cope, to hang on, to persevere. That is why so many do not stay; they would rather go out and play.

Yet, human nature, as disordered, disoriented, and imbalanced as it is, needs something to push against, something to wrestle with. St. Paul tells us, "My own actions bewilder me." Our creed enables us to cope with trouble, which can do devastating harm to a person. It can make him or her bitter, resentful, hard, cruel, despairing, fatalistic. But our creed gives the answers to those big question marks and enables us to share the cross of Christ at this moment in time in order to one day reach the zenith of his truth.

Remember, there is but one difference between a sinner and a saint. A sinner has a past and a saint has a future. May you mend the past and live in the present, so as to meet the future with its vision of God.